Introduction to Mary

Introduction to Mary

The Heart of Marian Doctrine and Devotion

Mark Miravalle, S.T.D.

Queenship
PUBLISHING COMPANY
P.O. Box 42028
Santa Barbara, CA 93140-2028

NIHIL OBSTAT
Father James Dunfee
Censor Librorum

IMPRIMATUR
Most Reverend Gilbert Sheldon
Bishop of Steubenville

January 12, 1993

Published by:
Queenship Publishing Company
P.O. Box 42028
Santa Barbara, CA 93140-2028

Printed in the United States of America

ISBN: 1-882972-06-6

Dedication

My wife and I dedicate this book to
Pope John Paul II:
a great Marian Vicar of Christ
and a contemporary hero.

Contents

Preface

Introduction to Mary comes as a response to repeated requests from mariology students, Marian conference members, and friends in and out of the Faith, for a contemporary book that would present the fundamental elements of both authentic Catholic doctrine and authentic Catholic devotion regarding Mary, the Mother of Jesus.

Far from being a comprehensive treatment of mariology (the study of the theology of Mary), the goal of this work is rather to synthesize Marian doctrine and devotion so as to serve as a basic introduction for both the parish study group and the college classroom, for both the inquiring non-Catholic and the long-standing Catholic. For a more extensive work on Marian doctrine and devotion rather than this concise Marian catechism, I would recommend *Mariology*, the three volume American work, edited by the late Juniper Carol, O.F.M. (Milwaukee: Bruce Publishing Co., 1955-61), or the Irish work by Fr. Michael O'Carroll C.S.Sp., *Theotokos: A Theological Encyclopedia of the Blessed Virgin Mary*, (Delaware: Michael Glazier, Inc., 1983).

We find ourselves in the midst of a Marian reawakening. But any authentic devotional renewal to the Mother of Jesus must be firmly rooted in the authentic doctrine regarding the Blessed Virgin Mary. I pray that this work will in some small way help to provide the proper doctrinal and devotional foundation to what many of our contemporaries see as a climax of our presently designated "Age of Mary."

Mark Miravalle, S.T.D.
Associate Professor of Theology and Mariology
Franciscan University of Steubenville
December 8, 1992

Acknowledgements

I wish to offer my heartfelt gratitude to my assistant, Miss Patricia Doepker, for her outstanding technical preparation of this text; to Sr. M. Regina Pacis, O.S.F., Associate Professor of Classics at Franciscan University of Steubenville for her invaluable proofing of the text; to Fr. William Most, esteemed contributor to mariology, for his proofing and helpful theological suggestions; and my greatest thanks to my chief consultant and principal supporter of this work, my wife, Beth.

Introduction

In discussing the person and role of Mary, Mother of Jesus, two extremes must always be avoided. The first extreme is what we call the extreme of *Marian excess*. This means to place the Blessed Virgin on the level of the divine, to ascribe to Mary a divine nature that would grant her equality with God Himself. This, of course, violates the revealed truth about the complete though exalted humanity of Mary. Although historically there have been very few occasions when the Mother of Jesus has been posed as a "goddess," nonetheless, it remains a Marian excess that is obviously a grave danger to the Faith.

The second extreme regarding the person and role of the Blessed Virgin is what we can call *Marian defect*. This means to minimize the role of the Blessed Virgin. What is meant by minimizing the role of Mary? This would be to ascribe to Mary the role of being only a "good disciple," a "sister in the Lord," a mere "physical channel of Jesus," but nothing beyond these.

Unfortunately it is this second extreme that is encountered more widely today. This extreme also violates the revealed truth of the role of the Blessed Virgin, for Mary is revealed, as we will talk about, both as intercessor and as Spiritual Mother. And to deny Mary the role of Spiritual Mother is to deny that aspect so central to her own identity and to her relationship with Christ and His Body, the Church.

As we shall see, examples of Mary's role as intercessor and
Spiritual Mother are clear in Scripture in such places as John 2:1
at the wedding of Cana, where Mary intercedes for the first
miracle of Jesus; as well as in John 19:26, where at the foot of the
Cross Mary is given the role of Spiritual Mother of John, the
beloved disciple, and all later disciples of the Lord.

We can find both of these extremes, Marian excess and
Marian defect, referred to in a statement from the Second
Vatican Council regarding the proper balance of Marian devo-
tion:

> It [the Council] strongly urges theologians and preachers
> of the word of God to be careful to refrain as much from
> all false exaggeration as from too summary an attitude in
> considering the special dignity of the Mother of God.
> Following the study of Sacred Scripture, the Fathers, the
> doctors and liturgy of the Church, and under the guid-
> ance of the Church's magisterium, let them rightly
> illustrate the duties and privileges of the Blessed Virgin
> which always refer to Christ, the source of all truth,
> sanctity, and devotion (*Lumen Gentium*, No. 67).[1]

The question must then be asked: What safeguards the
Christian from these two Marian extremes? What protects us
from a "false exaggeration" in Marian excess or "too summary an
attitude" in terms of Marian defect? The answer can only be the
authentic teaching office of the Church, the Magisterium. The
Magisterium is that teaching authority that Our Lord has
granted to His apostles and their successors, who, guided by the
Holy Spirit, have the crucial responsibility to safeguard, inter-
pret and serve Divine Revelation. And this is the revelation of
God as contained in both Sacred Tradition and Sacred Scripture.

Let us return to the words of the Second Vatican Council and see how God's full Word is revealed to us:

> In order that the full and living Gospel might always be preserved in the Church the apostles left bishops as their successors. They gave them "their own position of teaching authority." This sacred Tradition, then, and the sacred Scripture of both Testaments, are like a mirror, in which the Church, during its pilgrim journey here on earth, contemplates God.... Sacred Scripture is the speech of God as it is put down in writing under the breath of the Holy Spirit. And Tradition transmits in its entirety the Word of God which has been entrusted to the apostles...so that, enlightened by the Spirit of truth, they may faithfully preserve, expound and spread it abroad by their preaching. Thus it comes about that the Church does not draw her certainty about all revealed truths from the holy Scriptures alone. Hence, both Scripture and Tradition must be accepted and honored with equal feelings of devotion and reverence (*Dei Verbum*, Nos. 7, 9).

The Council points out that there is *one twinfold source* of God's revelation to humanity. The first aspect of this one twinfold source is Sacred Tradition. Sacred Tradition comprises the oral truths of God transmitted to the apostles and their successors (the pope and the bishops in union with the pope) under the guidance of the Holy Spirit. Vatican II describes Sacred Tradition in the following way:

> The apostolic preaching, which is expressed in a special way in the inspired books, was to be preserved in a continuous line of succession until the end of time. Hence, the apostles, in handing on what they themselves had received, warn the faithful to maintain the traditions

which they had learned either by word of mouth or by letter (cf. 2 Thes 2:15); and they warn them to fight hard for the faith that had been handed on to them once and for all (cf. Jude 3). What was handed on by the apostles comprises everything that serves to make the People of God live their lives in holiness and increase their faith. In this way the Church, in her doctrine, life, and worship, perpetuates and transmits to every generation all that she herself is, all that she believes (*Dei Verbum*, No. 8).

Sacred Scripture is the other aspect of that one twinfold source. Scripture comprises the divine truths of God written down under the inspiration of the Holy Spirit. The books of Scripture, as the Council notes, "firmly, faithfully and without error, teach that truth which God, for the sake of our salvation, wished to see confided to the sacred Scriptures" (*Dei Verbum*, No. 11).

The Second Vatican Council strongly points out that *both* Sacred Tradition and Sacred Scripture must receive *equal reverence* as aspects of God revealing Himself to humanity for our salvation. This understanding of the unity of Tradition and Scripture is very important in mariology (the study of the doctrine of Mary). For many of the truths that God has revealed about the Mother of Jesus are strongly contained in Sacred Tradition. But each Marian doctrine will also be mirrored at least implicitly in the apostolic preaching that came to be written down and today is known as the New Testament.

Now the role of safeguarding this deposit of faith in Scripture and Tradition is given to the Magisterium of the Church, the official teaching body. Again from Vatican II we read:

But the task of giving an authentic interpretation of the Word of God, whether in its written form or in the form of Tradition, has been entrusted to the living teaching office of the Church alone. Its authority in this matter is exercised in the name of Jesus Christ. Yet this Magisterium is not superior to the Word of God, but is its servant. It teaches only what has been handed on to it. At the divine command and with the help of the Holy Spirit, it listens to this devotedly, guards it with dedication and expounds it faithfully. All that it proposes for belief as being divinely revealed is drawn from this single deposit of faith [Tradition and Scripture] (*Dei Verbum*, No.10).

So, the Magisterium has the unique responsibility of safeguarding the deposit of faith that Christ gave to His Church which is guided by the Holy Spirit.

But why is a discussion about Divine Revelation so crucial to the doctrine and devotion of the Blessed Virgin Mary? To summarize in a single statement we could say that: "Marian orthopraxis is based on Marian orthodoxy." "Orthopraxis" is a Greek word which means the right practice, or correct devotion. "Orthodoxy" means the right or correct doctrine. Now when we apply this to mariology, devotion to Mary will be authentic only when it is based on authentic doctrine that comes from the Word of God entrusted to the Church. Marian devotion then will be authentic and, as such, an instrument of grace and ultimate union with Jesus Christ, only when it avoids both Marian excess and Marian defect. And to avoid extremes in Marian devotion, we must build our veneration of Mary soundly on authentic doctrine about Mary. This we receive from the Tradition and Scripture, as safeguarded by the Magisterium. The truth of Christ and His Church is the only legitimate foundation for a balance and legitimate devotion to the Mother of Jesus. In short, we can say that true devotion to Mary is based on the true doctrine about Mary.

On this journey of Marian doctrine and devotion we will

begin by discussing the nature of devotion to Mary and its origins in the first centuries of the Church. In Chapters Two and Three we will examine the doctrine of the Blessed Virgin as found in the sources of divine revelation and as taught by the Church's Magisterium.

After we have a solid understanding of authentic Marian doctrine, we will then examine the expression of authentic devotion to Mary. This will include chapter treatments on the Rosary, the greatest Marian prayer; consecration to Jesus through Mary, the crowning of Marian devotion; and Mary's message to the modern world through Marian private revelation. We will end with a discussion in "defense of Mary," responding to basic objections both to the doctrine and to the devotion of the Blessed Virgin.

Let us commence our journey of Marian doctrine and devotion with the most complete ancient Marian prayer recorded and dated at approximately 250 A.D. It is known as the *Sub Tuum Praesidium* (*"Under Your Protection"*):

> We fly to your patronage,
> O Holy Mother of God,
> despise not our petitions
> in our necessities,
> but deliver us from all danger,
> O ever glorious and blessed Virgin.

Notes

1. All Second Vatican Council references in text are quoted from Austin Flannery, O.P., *Vatican Council II, The Conciliar and Post Conciliar Documents*, (Northport NY: Costello Publishing Co., 1975).

chapter one

Devotion to Mary and Its Beginnings

What is Devotion to Mary?

We begin our inquiry into the person and role of Mary, Mother of Jesus, by addressing a most fundamental question: What is devotion to Mary?

To answer this question we must first make a basic theological distinction. Adoration, which is known as *latria* in classical theology, is the worship and homage that is rightly offered to God alone. It is the acknowledgement of excellence and perfection of an uncreated, divine person. It is the worship of the Creator that God alone deserves.

Veneration, known as *dulia* in classical theology, is the honor due to the excellence of a created person. This refers to the excellence exhibited by the created being who likewise deserves recognition and honor. We see a general example of veneration in events like the awarding of academic awards for excellence in school or the awarding of the olympic medals for excellence in sports. There is nothing contrary to the proper adoration of God when we offer the appropriate honor and recognition that created persons deserve based on achievement in excellence.[1]

Here a further clarification should be made regarding the use of the term "worship" in relation to the categories of adoration and veneration. Some schools of theology use the term "worship" to introduce *both* adoration and veneration. They would distinguish between "worship of adoration" and "worship of veneration." The word "worship" (in the same way the theological term "cult" is traditionally used) in these classical definitions was not at all synonymous with adoration, but could be used to introduce either adoration or veneration. Hence Catholic writers will sometimes use the term "worship" not to indicate adoration, but only the worship of veneration given to Mary and the saints. Confusion over the use of the term worship has led to the misunderstanding by some that Catholics offer adoration to Mary in a type of "Mariolatry," or Marian idolatry. Adoration to Mary has never been and will never be part of authentic Catholic doctrine and devotional life.

Under the category of veneration we see the honor and reverence that the saints rightly receive. Why? Because the saints manifested a true excellence in the pursuit and the attainment of Christian holiness, and in light of this excellence, Our Lord grants the saints in Heaven an ability to intercede for those on earth who are in the process of pursuing holiness. This is a basic principle of the mystical body of Christ and the communion of saints.

St. Thomas Aquinas points out a further truth regarding veneration of the saints. The devotion a person has to God's saints does not end with the saints themselves but rather reaches ultimately to God through the saints. This is an important element in properly understanding authentic Catholic devotion to the saints. For to give honor to the saint who has excelled in loving union with God is also to honor the object of his loving union: God Himself.

For example, if you offered special hospitality to the children of your long-time friends, then ultimately you are offering a sign of love to your long-time friends themselves. This is analogous to the veneration of saints. When we honor those who spent their life pursuing intimate union with God, we are also ultimately honoring God who is the object of their love.

In short, we can say it is pleasing to God and, ultimately, it gives Him glory when we honor those who excelled in love of Him. This is true about honoring the Mother of Jesus because of her special role in union with the Lord.

Within the general category of veneration we can speak of a unique level of veneration, an exalted level of honor that would be appropriate for honoring a created person whose excellence rises above that of every other created person. It is in this special level of veneration, classically called *hyperdulia*, that we find the proper devotion ascribed to the Blessed Virgin Mary.

Hyperdulia or special veneration of Mary remains completely different and inferior to adoration that is due to God alone. Devotion to Mary is never to rival in nature or in degree the adoration proper only to God. While veneration of the Blessed Virgin will always be inferior to the adoration given uniquely to God, it will always be superior and higher than devotion given to all other saints and angels.

This distinction between adoration and veneration and the unique veneration due to Mary is discussed by the Second Vatican Council. (Note the word "cult" as used in the text is interchangeable with "worship," referring here to veneration.):

> This cult [veneration of Mary], as it has always existed in the Church, for all its uniqueness, differs essentially from the cult of adoration, which is offered equally to the Incarnate Word and to the Father and the Holy Spirit, and it is most favorable to it. The various forms of piety towards the Mother of God, which the Church has approved within the limits of sound and orthodox doctrine, according to the dispositions and understand-

ing of the faithful, ensure that while the mother is honored, the Son through whom all things have their being (cf. Col 1:15-16) and in whom it has pleased the Father that all fullness should dwell (cf. Col 1:19) is rightly known, loved and glorified and his commandments are observed (*Lumen Gentium*, No. 66).

Mary's Exalted Devotion

Why does the Blessed Virgin deserve a unique and a higher level of devotion than all of the other saints and angels? There are at least three fundamental reasons an exalted devotion is appropriate to the Blessed Virgin of Nazareth.

First of all, Mary was granted by God a *fullness of grace*. From the greeting of the Angel Gabriel in the words, "Hail, full of grace, the Lord is with you" (Lk 1:28), we get an indication of God's special gift to Mary at the moment of conception. Mary received God's gift of being free from Original Sin from the first instant of her conception, preparing her to be the fitting Mother of the Word made flesh. This unique gift allowed a plentitude of grace for the Virgin, since this fullness of grace was not limited by a fallen nature.

All the other saints, on the other hand, have shared excellently in grace, but they did not have a plentitude of grace, due to the limitations of their fallen nature. Even St. John the Baptist, who was sanctified in the womb, as tradition tells us, started with a fallen nature, and then it was sanctified *in utero*. But St. John was not conceived with a nature like the Blessed Virgin's nature, a nature free from all stain of sin. Only a nature free from all stain of sin allows for a full plentitude of grace. Mary's fullness of grace rightly calls for special recognition and devotion.

Secondly, and most significantly, Mary alone had the privilege of being Mother of God the Son, Jesus Christ. The theological term is *theotokos*, which is Greek for "the God-bearer." Giving flesh to the "Word made flesh" grants Mary an excellence and a dignity beyond any other creature. We can imagine the intimate union and the spiritual effects of having God physically present in us for nine months and of giving Jesus His human nature. Because Mary as true Mother gave to Jesus what our mothers gave to us, a nature like her own, she is rightly the Mother of God.

Theologians have explained this by saying that the Blessed Virgin Mary alone had an "intrinsic relationship with the Hypostatic Union."[2] We remember that the Hypostatic Union is the union of the divine nature and the human nature in the one divine person of Jesus. Only Mary, of all creatures, had an interior and crucial role in Jesus' taking on human nature to become our Redeemer. Mary alone had an interior and essential participation in the Incarnation. This should not be underestimated, for to underestimate the role of Mary in God becoming man is also to underestimate the significance of God becoming man—the greatest event known in human history.

In short, the Blessed Mother gave the "carne" to the Incarnation. She gave flesh to the "Word made flesh" who "dwelt among us" (Jn 1:14). Only the Church in its fullness can ponder the unfathomable depths of how closely united Mary was, and is, with her divine Son.

Just having the physical presence of Jesus in the womb of Mary for nine months is like having the Eucharist constantly present within a person for nine complete months, constantly sanctifying its human tabernacle day and night by its spiritual and physical presence.

All other saints, even St. Joseph, no matter how closely associated with the Incarnation, had at best an external relationship with God becoming man for our salvation. (More will be discussed concerning the Marian doctrines of the Immaculate

Conception and Divine Motherhood in Chapter 2.)

The third reason for an exalted devotion to the Mother of Jesus is Mary's perfect obedience to the will of God throughout her life on earth. Mary's *fiat*, her *yes* to the will of God, was her response to God's will and not only at the Annunciation (cf. Luke 1:38) but throughout her earthly life. By cooperating with her God-given enmity against Satan prophesied in Genesis (Gen 3:15), her complete opposition to the serpent and to his seed of sin, Mary never said no to the manifest will of God during her earthly life. It is for this reason that the Council of Trent, the universal council of the Church in the sixteenth century, declared: "No justified person can for his whole life avoid all sins, even venial sins, except on the grounds of a special privilege from God, such as the Church holds was given to the Blessed Virgin" (Council of Trent, DS, 833). Only one creature was given this special privilege to commit neither Original Sin nor personal sin during her earthly life. Because of her perfect obedience to God's will, she is the perfect model of all Christian virtue. She is the perfect model not only of obedience but also of humility, of faith, hope and charity. She is referred to as "Model of the Church" as well as "Mother of the Church." Because of her being the perfect model of Christian virtue Mary properly deserves both our special devotion and our special imitation.

For these three reasons and several more, the Blessed Virgin rightly receives a singular and unique place of special devotion in the Church which is higher than that of the saints and angels, but always humbly below the adoration due to God alone. This is summarized in the words of Vatican II:

> Joined to Christ the head and in communion with all his saints, the faithful must in the first place reverence the memory "of the glorious ever Virgin Mary, Mother of God and of our Lord Jesus Christ" (*Lumen Gentium*, No. 52).

and:

> Mary has by grace been exalted above all angels and men
> to a place second only to her Son, as the most holy
> mother of God who was involved in the mysteries of
> Christ: she is rightly honored by a special cult [devotion]
> in the Church (*Lumen Gentium*, No. 66).

Since God has willed that the Blessed Virgin have such an
important role in the work of God becoming man and saving the
human family, devotion to Mary then is not arbitrary nor is it
extraordinary. Devotion to Mary is, rather, an ordinary part of
the Christian journey to Christ and eternal salvation. Pope St.
Pius X, the pontiff at the beginning of the twentieth century,
confirms this truth about the singular privilege of Mary being
not from necessity, but nonetheless from the manifest will of
God:

> God could have given us the Redeemer of the human
> race and the Founder of the Faith in another way than
> through the Virgin, but since Divine Providence has
> been pleased that we should have the God-man through
> Mary, who conceived Him by the Holy Spirit and bore
> Him in her womb, it remains for us to receive Christ only
> through the hands of Mary (*Ad diem illum*).

As is true of so many of the aspects of our faith, including our
very salvation, the role of the Blessed Virgin and the proper
devotion that comes as a result of her role are not from necessity,
but rather from the manifest will of God whose divine ways are
perfect. God did not have to use the Blessed Mother either in
terms of the Incarnation or in terms of Redemption. But the fact
of divine revelation is that it was God's will that Mary have this
central role. And because it was God's will, it calls for an

appropriate response by the human family: a response of special devotion to the woman and mother chosen to be at the heart of the mysteries of the Incarnation and Redemption.

Devotion to Mary is not on the same level as a preferred devotion to an individual saint, like St. Jude, St. Therese or St. Francis, as valuable and praiseworthy as devotions to individual saints are. Rather, devotion to Mary is beyond devotion to all other saints, and it should be a universal step on the path to Christ, since her role in Jesus' becoming man and saving humanity had a universal impact on the world.

But again, this superior devotion to the Blessed Mother will never take away the primacy or the dignity of Jesus Christ as the one Savior and Redeemer. Her role and her corresponding devotion will always be subordinate to the adoration proper to Jesus Christ. St. Louis Marie de Montfort, possibly the Church's greatest Marian enthusiast of the last five hundred years, illustrates this point well in his very first paragraph of the papally endorsed *True Devotion to Mary*:

> I avow, with all the Church, that Mary, being a mere creature that has come from the hands of the Most High, is in comparison with His Infinite Majesty less than an atom; or rather, she is nothing at all, because only He is "He who is" (Ex. 3:14); consequently that grand Lord, always independent and sufficient to Himself, never had, and has not now, any absolute need of the holy Virgin for the accomplishment of His glory. He has but to will in order to do everything.

> Nevertheless, I say that, things being as they are now— that is, God having willed to commence and complete His greatest works by the most holy Virgin ever since He created her—we may well think He will not change His conduct in the eternal ages.[3]

Therefore, not from necessity but from God's manifest will are derived both Mary's role in salvation and our appropriate corresponding devotion to her.

Historical Beginnings of Devotion to Mary

Mary in Scripture

Here we want to look briefly at the beginnings of Marian devotion from its foreshadowings in the Old Testament and its revelation in the New Testament, to its beginning in the infant Church, and its growth up to the universal (or ecumenical) Church Council of Ephesus (A.D. 431). We will see that after the Council of Ephesus where Mary is proclaimed "Mother of God," the history of Marian devotion is basically as widespread and as all encompassing as the history of Western civilization itself.

Mary Foreshadowed in the Old Testament

Like all central mysteries of the Catholic faith, the doctrine and the devotion to the Blessed Virgin started in seed form, doctrinal seeds planted by the Divine Sower. These doctrinal and devotional seeds are contained in divine revelation and have developed and blossomed over time in the dynamic life of the living Church.

The role of Mary, like other Catholic truths, was foreshadowed in the Old Testament. In Genesis, the very first book of the Old Testament, which has been called the "Protoevangelicum" meaning "first gospel," the "woman" and the "serpent" are put in "enmity": "I will put enmity between you [the serpent] and the woman, and between your seed and her seed; he shall bruise your head, and you shall bruise his heel" (Gen 3:15).

Enmity means a complete and entire mutual opposition. Since the seed of the woman is Christ the Redeemer, then the woman must also refer to the Blessed Virgin who, with her Son, has complete enmity against Satan and against sin.

The prophecy of Isaiah 7:14 speaks of the "Virgin-Mother of Emmanuel": "Therefore the Lord himself will give you a sign. Behold, a virgin shall conceive and bear a son, and his name shall be called Emmanuel." Later in Isaiah, Emmanuel is referred to as the future Savior of His people (Is 8:8-9).

We have the prophecy of Micah 5:2-3 which foretells the birth of the Savior in Bethlehem from a woman who will "bring forth" the "ruler of Israel":

> But you, O Bethlehem Ephrathah, are a little one among the thousands of Judah, from you shall come forth for me one who is to be the ruler in Israel, and his going forth is from the beginning, from the days of eternity. Therefore he shall give them up until the time when she who is in travail shall bring forth, then the rest of his brethren shall return to Israel.

The mother, introduced so suddenly in Micah and so specifically designated without a husband, conveys, according to the commentaries of several mariologists, the same virginal sense as we see in Isaiah 7:14. The fact that she is so strongly and clearly designated as a woman without a husband represents at least an implicit reference to that same virgin birth.

Numerous other models or types of the Blessed Virgin Mary are present in the Old Testament. Pope Pius IX, in his dogmatic definition of the Immaculate Conception in 1854, refers to several of these Old Testament types of Mary which were recognized by the early Church Fathers themselves. Mary was seen as the *Ark of Noah* built by divine command who escaped the effects of sin (Gen 6:9). *Jacob's Ladder* that reached from earth to Heaven and that angels used to ascend and descend, was seen as a sign of the future intercession of the Blessed Virgin (Gen 28:12). The Fathers saw the *Burning Bush* of Moses as a type of Mary because it held the presence of God but without corruption (Ex 3:1). From the Canticle of Canticles Mary is depicted in the *impenetrable tower of David* and in the *enclosed and inviolable garden* (Cant 4:4,12). Also the *Temple of God* in 1 Kings 8 represented a sanctified house of God which foreshadowed Mary as the future tabernacle of Jesus.[4]

The *Ark of the Covenant* is a strong model of Mary as that chosen special place that held the presence of God (cf. Gen 6:14; Ex 37:1), as well as the several references to *created wisdom* in the book of Wisdom.

These Old Testament references and several more illustrate the repeated foreshadowing of the Mother of the Redeemer, both in terms of her intercession and in terms of her virginal and pure nature. So, we see that the Old Testament is very rich in foretelling, through models and types, the future role of the Mother of Jesus.

As the Second Vatican Council confirms:

[S]he is already prophetically foreshadowed in the promise of victory over the serpent which was given to our first parents after their fall into sin (cf. Gen 3:15). Likewise, she is the virgin who shall conceive and bear a son, whose name shall be called Emmanuel (cf. Is 7:14; Mic 5:2-3; Mt 1:22-23). She stands out among the poor and humble of the Lord, who confidently hope for and receive salvation from him. After a long period of waiting the times are fulfilled in her, the exalted Daughter of Sion and the new plan of salvation is established, when the Son of God has taken human nature from her, that he might in the mysteries of his flesh free man from sin (*Lumen Gentium*, No. 55).

Mary in the New Testament

The New Testament manifests several revealed truths about the Blessed Virgin that are both centrally positioned and theologically profound. The citations of Mary in the New Testament surround the central Christian mysteries revealed in the Gospel. The question may be asked, "Why is there not more of a *developed* treatment of Mary and her devotion in the New Testament?" For several reasons it is important that Mary have a select presence in the New Testament.

The complete attention of the faithful in the infant years of the one Church of Christ had first to be directed pre-eminently to Jesus Christ Himself. The proper adoration of Jesus has to be established before any secondary veneration of Mary would be appropriate or fitting. Her honor, of course, arises first and foremost from her being the Mother of Jesus.

Further, the comparative obscurity of Mary was important to avoid any rash conclusion of an all too human conception of Jesus. In other words, to avoid concluding that the "wise, pure and holy" Jesus was simply the product of a very "wise, pure and holy" mother. Mary's obscurity protected and focused the attention of the Apostolic Church towards the single primacy of Jesus and His heavenly origins.

Moreover, it was important that during Mary's lifetime her humility was rightly respected and protected. Mary was to be the perpetual example of hidden holiness, of interior sanctity—a model for Christians of all future ages. For these reasons it was very fitting that Mary, as the humble handmaid of the Lord, not have more development in the New Testament, so as not to diminish the primacy of her Son and His own example.

Nevertheless, the revealed truths about Mary's unique privilege with her Son in the New Testament can be seen in "seed form" from the praises that came from the Angel Gabriel and Elizabeth (Lk 1:28f,42), to the words of Jesus on the Cross (Jn 19:26), to John's description of her glory in Revelation (Rev 12). These and other doctrinal seeds offer more than enough scriptural basis for an authentic devotion to Mary. Although these New Testament passages referring to Mary will be discussed in greater detail as they arise in the upcoming treatment on Marian doctrine and devotion, let us quickly survey some of the principal New Testament citings about the Blessed Virgin.

In the first two chapters of St. Luke's Gospel (referred to as "Our Lady's Gospel" because of its many Marian references), we can follow the pattern of the Joyful Mysteries of the Rosary to summarize the chief Marian citations:

> • *The Annunciation* (Lk 1:26-38), where the words of the Angel Gabriel, "Hail, full of grace, the Lord is with you" (Lk 1:28), greet Mary and go on to announce Mary as the chosen Mother of the Savior.
> • *The Visitation* (Lk 1:39-56) of Mary to Elizabeth where, "when Elizabeth heard the greeting of Mary, the babe in her womb leapt and she was filled with the Holy Spirit" (Lk 1:41), and where Mary proclaims her magnificat that "all generations will call me blessed" (Lk 1:48).
> • *The Nativity* (Lk 2:4-20) of Jesus, where Mary "brought forth her first-born Son and wrapped him in swaddling clothes" (Lk 2:7).
> • *The Presentation* (Lk 2:22-38) of the Infant Jesus in the Temple by Mary and Joseph, where the prophetic words of Simeon inform Mary that "a sword will pierce your own heart too" (Lk 2:35).
> • *The Finding of the Child Jesus in the Temple* (Lk 2:41-52), where, after Jesus informs Mary and Joseph that "I must be about my Father's business" (Lk 2:49), Mary

"kept all these things pondering them in her heart"
(Lk 2:51).

The Gospel of St. Matthew adds several more Marian
scriptural references:

• *The betrothal of Mary* (Mt 1:18) to Joseph.
• *The ordeal of Joseph* (Mt 1:20) concerning the virgin
conception of Jesus in Mary, where the angel tells Joseph
"do not fear to take Mary as your wife, for that which is
conceived of her is of the Holy Spirit."
• *The arrival of the Magi* (Mt 2:1-12), the wise men, and
how "going into the house they saw the Child with Mary
his Mother, and they fell down and worshipped him"
(Mt 2:11).
• *The flight of the Holy Family into Egypt* (Mt 2:13-18),
where Joseph was again instructed by a dream to "take
the Child and his Mother and flee into Egypt" (Mt 2:13).
• *The return into Israel* (Mt 2:19-23), where Joseph is
instructed to "rise, take the Child and his Mother, and go
to the land of Israel, for those who sought the Child's life
are dead" (Mt 2:20).

Note that many of these infancy references repeatedly bespeak
the unity of "the Child and his Mother" as a sign of the profound
union of Jesus and Mary that would continue for all time.

Beyond the infancy narratives of St. Luke and St. Matthew
other principal Marian Scripture references include:

• *The wedding at Cana* (Jn 2:1-11) where, through
Mary's intercession, Jesus performs His first miracle
beginning His public ministry, and where the resound-
ing Marian words are spoken that continue to echo
today: "Do whatever he tells you" (Jn 2:5).

• *Mary at the foot of the Cross* (Jn 19:25-27) where Mary is given to John and to all "beloved disciples" as Spiritual Mother: "Woman, behold thy Son...Son behold thy Mother" (Jn 19:26-27).

• *The presence of Mary in the Upper Room* (Acts 1:13-2:4) awaiting the events of Pentecost where, "Mary, the Mother of Jesus" (Acts 1:14) is seen at the heart of the infant Church after the Resurrection and Ascension of her Son.

• *Marian reference of Galatians 4:4*, where St. Paul tells us the Savior was "born of a woman" (Gal 4:4). The term "woman" spans Marian references throughout the Scriptures from the woman in enmity with the serpent (Gen 3:15) in the first book of the Bible to the "woman clothed with the sun" (Rev 12:1) in the last book of the Bible.

• *Marian reference of Revelation 12:1* where Mary, seen also as a type of the Church, is described in her assumed and crowned glory, as "a woman clothed with the sun with the moon under her feet and on her head a crown of twelve stars" (Rev 12:1).

In summary, we can see that Mary's place in Sacred Scripture is select but profound and certainly provides the necessary doctrinal grounds for the corresponding devotion that was to develop gradually in the early Church.

Mary in the Early Church

As in Scripture, so too in the infant Church, we see the attention of the faithful rightfully focused first and foremost on Jesus Christ. Without establishing the primacy of Jesus, neither devotion to His Mother nor even the existence of His Body the Church, is possible. Nonetheless, the beginnings of acknowledgement and devotion to the Mother of Jesus is present from apostolic times in the living Tradition of the early Church.

The first historic indications of the existing veneration of Mary carried on from the Apostolic Church is present in the Roman catacombs. As early as the end of the first century to the first half of the second century, Mary is depicted in frescos in the Roman catacombs both with and without her divine Son. Mary is depicted as a model of virginity with her Son; at the Annunciation; and at the adoration of the Magi; and as the *orans*, the woman of prayer.

A very significant fresco found in the catacombs of St. Agnes depicts Mary situated between St. Peter and St. Paul with her arms outstretched to both. This fresco is the earliest symbol of Mary as "Mother of the Church." Whenever St. Peter and St. Paul are shown together, it is symbolic of the one Church of Christ, a Church of authority and evangelization, a Church for both Jew and Gentile. Mary's prominent position between Sts. Peter and Paul illustrates the recognition by the Apostolic Church of the maternal centrality of the Savior's Mother in His prevailing Church.

It is also clear from the number of representations of the Blessed Virgin and their locations in the catacombs that Mary was seen not only as an historical person but also as a sign of protection, of defense, and of intercession. Her image was present on tombs, as well as on the large central vaults of the catacombs. Clearly, the early Christians dwelling in the catacombs prayed to Mary as intercessor to her Son for special protection and for motherly assistance. So we see as early as the first century to the first half of the second century that Mary's role as Spiritual Mother and intercessor was recognized and invoked.[5]

The early Church Fathers, also by the middle of the second century, considered the primary theological role of the Blessed Virgin as the "New Eve." What was the basic understanding of

Mary as the "New Eve" in the early Church? Eve, the original "mother of the living," had played an instrumental though secondary role in the sin of Adam which resulted in the tragic fall of humanity from God's grace. But Mary, as the new Mother of the living, played an instrumental though secondary role to Jesus, the New Adam, in redeeming and restoring the life of grace to the human family. This maternal role in restoring grace to the human family manifests the role of Mary as both intercessor and Spiritual Mother.

Let us look at a few citations from the early Church Fathers that manifest this growing understanding of Mary's spiritual and maternal role as the "New Eve," who as the "new Mother of the living," participates with Christ in restoring grace to the human family.

St. Justin Martyr (d.165), the early Church's first great apologist, describes Mary as the "obedient virgin" in contrast to Eve, the "disobedient virgin":

[The Son of God] became man through the Virgin that the disobedience caused by the serpent might be destroyed in the same way in which it had originated. For Eve, while a virgin incorrupt, conceived the word which proceeded from the serpent, and brought forth disobedience and death. But the Virgin Mary was filled with faith and joy when the Angel Gabriel told her the glad tidings.... And through her was he born.... [6]

St. Irenaeus of Lyon (d.202), great defender of orthodoxy and possibly the first true mariologist, establishes Mary as the New Eve who participates with Jesus Christ in the work of salvation:

Just as Eve, wife of Adam, yet still a virgin, became by her disobedience the cause of death for herself and the whole human race, so Mary, too, espoused yet a Virgin, became by her obedience the cause of salvation for herself and the whole human race....And so it was that the knot of Eve's disobedience was loosed by Mary's obedience. For what the virgin Eve bound fast by her refusal to believe, this the Virgin Mary unbound by her belief.[7]

Later, St. Ambrose (d.397) further develops the New Eve understanding:

It was through a man and woman that flesh was cast from Paradise; it was through a virgin that flesh was linked to God....Eve is called mother of the human race, but Mary Mother of salvation.[8]

And St. Jerome (d.420) neatly summarizes this whole understanding of the New Eve in the pithy expression, "death through Eve, life through Mary."[9]

The Second Vatican Council confirms this early understanding of Mary as the "New Eve" by the Church Fathers:

Rightly, therefore, the Fathers see Mary not merely as passively engaged by God, but as freely cooperating in the work of man's salvation through faith and obedience....Hence not a few of the early Fathers gladly assert with him [Irenaeus] in their preaching: "the knot of Eve's disobedience was untied by Mary's obedience: what the virgin Eve bound by her disbelief, Mary loosened by her faith." Comparing Mary with Eve, they call her "Mother of the living" and frequently claim: "death through Eve, life through Mary" (*Lumen Gentium*, No. 56).

The first centuries of the Church provide us with examples

of direct prayer to Mary as a means of intercession to the graces and protection of her Son.

For St. Irenaeus, Mary is an interceding helper (advocate) for Eve and for her salvation. St. Gregory Thaumatengus (d.350) depicts Mary in Heaven interceding for those on earth.

St. Ephraem (d.373), a great Eastern doctor of the Blessed Virgin, has direct address to the Blessed Virgin in several Marian sermons. And direct prayer to Mary is clearly found in a sermon of the great Eastern Father, St. Gregory Nazianzen (330-389).[10]

Within the last part of the fourth century and the beginning of the fifth, we have numerous explicit examples of direct prayer to Mary; for example in the writings of St. Ambrose, who was later to have his converting influence on St. Augustine, as well as in the Eastern Father, St. Epiphanius.

The most complete ancient prayer to the Blessed Mother preserved is the *Sub Tuum Praesidium*, which means *Under Your Protection*. It is dated approximately 250 A.D. Note the depth of understanding by the third century Church of Mary as having the power to intercede for spiritual protection:

> We fly to your patronage,
> O holy Mother of God,
> despise not our petitions
> in our necessities,
> but deliver us from all dangers.
> O ever glorious and blessed Virgin.

The early Christians knew that Mary could be trusted to intercede for protection in the midst of their trials, that the Mother of Jesus was a means of hope against dangers both spiritual and temporal.

By the time of the Council of Ephesus in 431 A.D., where Mary is declared the "Mother of God," we have cathedrals dedicated to her in the central ecclesial locations of Rome,

Jerusalem and Constantinople.

After the Council of Ephesus, we see a tremendous flourishing of devotion to the Blessed Virgin both in the East and the West, the quantity and quality of which would exceed the most comprehensive study. Such an effort would be similar to trying to document the overall development of Western civilization itself. Marian prayers, Marian liturgical feast days, Marian icons, Marian paintings, Marian artwork became ubiquitous throughout the Christian world after the Council of Ephesus in 431 A.D.

The Second Vatican Council attests to this tremendous flourishing of Marian devotion from the early Church onward:

> From the earliest times the Blessed Virgin is honored under the title of Mother of God, whose protection the faithful take refuge together in prayer in all their perils and needs. Accordingly, following the Council of Ephesus, there was a remarkable growth in the cult of the People of God towards Mary, in veneration and love, in invocation and imitation, according to her own prophetic words: "all generations shall call me blessed, because he that is mighty hath done great things to me (Lk 1:48) (*Lumen Gentium*, No. 66).

Historians have further testified to the vast influence of Marian devotion upon the overall development of Western civilization. The British historian, Kenneth Clark, himself not Catholic, describes in his excellent work, *Civilization*, the dramatic effect of devotion to the Blessed Virgin on Western civilization. He describes Mary as

> the supreme protectress of civilization. She had taught a race of tough and ruthless barbarians the virtues of tenderness and compassion. The great cathedrals of the

Middle Ages were her dwelling places upon earth...in the Renaissance, while remaining Queen of Heaven, she became also the human Mother in whom everyone could recognize qualities of warmth and love and approachability....[T]he all-male religions [a reference to Israel, Islam and the Protestant North] have produced no religious imagery—in most cases have positively forbidden it. The great religious art of the world is deeply involved in the female principle.[11]

Along with the impact of devotion to Mary on Western civilization, the fruitful effects of Marian devotion on the proper dignity of woman has also been historically verified. The noted historian, William Lecky, who was neither Catholic nor Christian but a self-professed rationalist, made these comments about the influence of Mary on the West:

The world is governed by its ideals, and seldom or never has there been one which has exercised a more salutary influence than the medieval concept of the Virgin. For the first time woman was elevated to her rightful position, and the sanctity of weakness was recognized, as well as the sanctity of sorrow.

No longer the slave or toy of man, no longer associated only with ideas of degradation and of sensuality, woman rose, in the person of the Virgin Mother, into a new sphere, and became the object of reverential homage, of which antiquity had no conception.... A new type of character was called into being; a new kind of admiration was fostered. Into a harsh and ignorant and benighted age, this ideal type infused a conception of gentleness and purity, unknown to the proudest civilizations of the past.

In the pages of living tenderness, which many a monkish
writer has left in honor of his celestial patron; in the
millions who, in many lands and in many ages, have
sought to mold their characters into her image; in those
holy maidens who, for love of Mary, have separated
themselves from all glories and pleasures of the world, to
seek in fastings and vigils and humble charity to render
themselves worthy of her benedictions; in the new sense
of honor, in the chivalrous respect, in the softening of
manners, in the refinement of tastes displayed in all
walks of society; in these and in many other ways we
detect the influence of the Virgin. All that was best in
Europe clustered around it, and it is the origin of many
of the purest elements of our civilization.[12]

Possibly, as no other besides her Son, the Mother of Jesus and
the rightful devotion granted to her throughout the ages have
borne fruit in a proper respect for person, a proper respect for the
unique dignity of woman, and a new cultivation of all that is
good in Western civilization.

In summary, then, we can say that authentic devotion to the
Mother of Jesus, which is foreshadowed in the Old Testament
and divinely planted in the New Testament, began its authentic
growth in the early Church and, since the fifth century, has
flourished vivaciously throughout the Christian world.

We can conclude with the words of Dante from the classic
The Divine Comedy which typifies well the strength of devotion
to the Blessed Virgin that has been evidenced throughout the
history of the Church: "...with living mortals you are a living
spring of hope. Lady, you are so great and have such worth, that
if anyone seeks out grace and flies not to thee, his longing is like
flight without wings."[13]

Notes

1. For distinction of *latria*, *dulia*, and *hyperdulia*, cf. St. Thomas Aquinas, *Summa Theologica*, II-II, Q 84, a. 1; Q 304, a. 1-4.
2. Cf. Suarez, S.J., *Disputationes*, 10, all III.
3. St. Louis Marie De Montfort, *True Devotion to Mary*, Chapter 1, p.1.
4. Cf. Pius IX, *Ineffabilis Deus*, 1854.
5. Cf. Murphy, "Origin and Nature of Marian Cult" in Carol, ed., *Mariology*, Vol. III, (Milwaukee: Bruce, 1961), pp. 1-20.
6. St. Justin Martyr, *Dialogue with Trypho*, ch. 100, *Patrologia Graeca* (PG) Migne, 6, 709-712.
7. St. Irenaeus, *Adversus haereses*, Bk. 3, pg. 32, I; PG 7, 958-959.
8. St. Ambrose, *Epist.* 63, n. 33, *Patrologia Latina* (PL) Migne, 16, 1249-1250; Sermon 45, n. 4; PL, 17, 716.
9. St. Jerome, *Epist.* 22, n. 21, PL 22, 408; cf. Walter Burghart, S.J. "Mary in Western Patristic Thought," *Mariology*, Vol. I, 1955.
10. Murphy, *Mariology*, III, p. 6.
11. Kenneth Clark, *Civilization* as quoted in Dan Lyons, *The Role of Mary Through the Centuries*, Washington, New Jersey, World Apostolate of Fatima.
12. Cf. Lyons, *The Role of Mary Through the Centuries*.
13. Dante, "Paradiso" in *The Divine Comedy*, Canto 33.

chapter two

The Person of Mary in Doctrine

The doctrine of the Blessed Virgin Mary reveals the role of the Mother of Jesus in relation to Christ and His Church. Authentic doctrine regarding Mary is, in fact, a revelation of the person of Mary herself. That is why by truly understanding *what* Mary's role is in God's work of redemption, we can know better *who* Mary is. Authentic love of Mary must be based on the *truth* about Mary.

This matter of Mary's self-revelation is exemplified at Lourdes during her apparitions in 1858. To Bernadette's question concerning who she was, Mary responded, "I am the Immaculate Conception."

In this chapter we will look at four of the five central Catholic truths (known as *de fide* doctrines) regarding the Blessed Virgin Mary: her *Motherhood of God*, her *Immaculate Conception*, her *Perpetual Virginity*, and her *Assumption*. In the following chapter, we will see how these four revealed truths converge in her role as *Spiritual Mother* of all humanity, a God-given role that is fulfilled in her function as Co-redemptrix and Mediatrix of graces.

Mother of God

The first and foremost revealed truth about Mary from which all her other roles and all her other honors flow is that Mary is the Mother of God. This doctrine proclaims that the Virgin Mary is true Mother of Jesus Christ who is God the Son made man. The doctrine of Mary's divine motherhood, as it is commonly referred to, is explicitly revealed in Sacred Scripture. At the Annunciation the Angel Gabriel declares to Mary: "Behold, you shall conceive in your womb and shall bring forth a son, and you shall call his name Jesus...;therefore, the holy one who shall be born of you shall be called Son of God" (Lk 1:31; Lk 1:35).

The angelic message which originates from God Himself attests that Mary is true Mother of Jesus and secondly, that Jesus is true Son of God. From these words of the angel, we can derive the following simple theological syllogism: Mary is Mother of Jesus; Jesus is God; therefore, Mary is Mother of God. Since Jesus is truly God the Son, and Mary is repeatedly referred to in Scripture as the "Mother of Jesus" (cf. Mt 2:13, 2:20; Jn 2:1,3; Acts 1:14, etc.), then Mary must be true Mother of God made man.

In Tradition we first find the revealed truth of Mary's divine motherhood in the Apostles' Creed. This great formula of the essential doctrinal beliefs of the early Church professes faith in "Jesus Christ, His only Son, our Lord, who was conceived by the Holy Spirit, born of the Virgin Mary."

From the teaching authority of the Church, we have the great Marian event of the third ecumenical council of the Church, the Council of Ephesus in 431 A.D. We remember that the ecumenical councils are those general assemblies of bishops who, with the authority and confirmation of the pope, and guided by the Holy Spirit, teach and define doctrine as found in divine revelation that is binding on the universal Church (hence, the name *ecumenical* or *general* council).

The ecumenical Council of Ephesus in 431 declared Mary as the Mother of God or *Theotokos* (literally the "God-bearer"). The Council approved the teaching of St. Cyril of Alexandria who, against the errors of Nestorius, declared:

> If anyone does not confess that the Emmanuel [Christ] in truth is God and that on this account the Holy Virgin is the Mother of God [Theotokos] in as much as she gave birth to the Word of God made flesh...let him be anathema (Council of Ephesus, DS 113).

Nestorius refused to call Mary "Mother of God" not primarily because of a mariological error, but because of a Christological error (an error concerning the true doctrine of Jesus).

Nestorius erroneously divided the one person of Jesus Christ into two separate persons, and thus Mary would be Mother only of the "human person of Jesus," and not the Mother of God. The Ephesus definition of Mary as the *Theotokos* is actually a protection of the revealed truth about Jesus: that Jesus is one divine person with two natures, one divine nature and one human nature, and that the two natures are inseparably united in the one and only one divine person of Jesus. We see then at Ephesus a case in point of the truth that authentic Marian doctrine will always protect and safeguard authentic doctrine about Jesus Christ. Several times in the early Church, when there was a statement about Our Lord Jesus which lacked clarity concerning its ramifications, it was applied to the Mother of Jesus, whereby it became clear that the Christological statement was incompatible with authentic Catholic doctrine. It is in this way that Marian doctrine safeguards the true doctrine about Jesus Christ.

Motherhood

To have an accurate understanding of Mary as Mother of God we must first have a clear understanding of the nature of motherhood itself. How do we define motherhood?

Motherhood is the act of a woman giving to her offspring the same type of nature that she herself has. This gift of nature is given through the process of conception, growth or gestation, and birth. The fruit of this process, which we may call maternal generation, is the whole child, the son or daughter, and not only the physical body.

For example, we rightly say that St. Elizabeth is the "mother" of St. John the Baptist, that is, mother of the complete person, not just of St. John's body. This is a true statement even though we know that Elizabeth did not give John his soul which is created and infused directly by God. Motherhood then refers to the gift of like nature, with the fruit of motherhood always including the entire person.

It is in this same accurate sense that Mary is rightly called the "Mother of God." What precisely does Mary give Jesus in the act of motherhood? First of all, let us establish what she did not give Jesus. Mary did not give Jesus His divine nature, nor did Mary give Jesus His divine personhood. Both of these aspects of Our Lord, in His divinity, existed from all eternity. But, "when in the fullness of time, God sent his son born of a woman" (Gal 4:4), Mary gave Jesus a human nature identical to her own, in the same way that each of our human mothers gave each of us a human nature. Since the human nature of Jesus is inseparably united to His divine nature in the one person of Christ, we correctly say that Mary gave birth to a Son who is truly God and, through Mary, truly man. In short, Mary gave flesh to the Word made flesh and is rightfully proclaimed "Mother of God."[1]

It is for this reason that Jesus is called both "Son of God" and "Son of Mary." Jesus is Son of the Father, since His divine nature was generated (not made) by the Father from all eternity. Jesus is Son of Mary since His human nature was given to Him by Mary, His earthly Mother.

The truth of Mary's divine motherhood and its corresponding dignity are found in these words of the Second Vatican Council:

> [S]he is endowed with the high office and dignity of the Mother of the Son of God, and therefore she is also the beloved daughter of the Father and the temple of the Holy Spirit. Because of this gift of sublime grace she far surpasses all creatures, both in heaven and on earth (*Lumen Gentium*, No. 53).

The Immaculate Conception

The second central Marian doctrine is the doctrine of the Immaculate Conception. This doctrine, which received the added certainty of an infallible definition by Pope Pius IX in 1854, proclaims that Mary was conceived without any stain of Original Sin. Before examining the full solemn pronouncement of Pope Pius IX, which was issued with the papal charism of being protected from error by the power of the Holy Spirit, let us first examine the revealed seeds of this doctrine as they are contained in Scripture and Tradition.

From Sacred Scripture we have at least two passages of the Bible that present the implicit seed of the revealed truth of Mary's Immaculate Conception.

In Genesis 3:15, after Adam and Eve committed Original Sin, God addresses Satan, who is represented by the serpent: "I will put enmity between you and the woman and between your seed and her seed; he[2] shall crush your head, and you shall lie in wait for his heel." Since the "seed" of the woman is Jesus Christ, who is to crush Satan victoriously in the redemption, then the woman must in fact refer to Mary, Mother of the Redeemer.

The word "enmity," which is rich in meaning in this passage, signifies "in opposition to." The enmity established between the "seed" of the woman, which is Jesus, and the "seed" of the serpent, which is sin, and all evil angels and humans, is in absolute and complete opposition, because there is absolute and complete opposition between Jesus and all evil. In other words, the seed of the woman and the seed of Satan have to be in complete and total opposition to each other as depicted in the term "enmity."

Further in the passage we see the identical God-given opposition or enmity given and proclaimed by God between the woman, Mary, and the serpent, Satan. Mary is given the same absolute and perpetual opposition to Satan as Jesus possesses in relation to sin. It is for this reason that Mary could not have received a fallen nature as a result of Original Sin. Any participation in the effects of Original Sin would place the Mother of Jesus in at least partial participation with Satan and sin, thereby destroying the complete God-given opposition as revealed in Genesis 3.

The opposition between Jesus and sin is paralleled by the opposition between the woman, Mary, and the serpent, Satan. Again, this tells us that Mary could not participate in the fallen nature because that would mean participating, at least partially, in the domain of sin, a reality to which God gave Mary complete opposition.

From the New Testament the principal scriptural seed for the Immaculate Conception is revealed in the inspired words of the Angel Gabriel, "Hail, full of grace, the Lord is with you" (Lk 1:28). In the angelic greeting, Mary's name is nowhere used. Rather, the title "full of grace" is used as a substitute for Mary's name by the angelic messenger of God. These angelic words refer to a fullness of grace, a plentitude of grace that is part of Mary's very nature. So much is Mary's very being full of grace that this title serves to identify Mary in place of her own name. It is also true that no person with a fallen nature could possess a fullness of grace, a plentitude of grace, appropriate only for the woman who was to give God the Son an identical, immaculate human nature. Mary was conceived in providence to be the woman who would give her same immaculate nature to God when God became man. Certainly we can see the fittingness in God receiving a human nature from a human mother, and receiving an immaculate nature from a truly immaculate mother.

In the Greek text of Luke 1:28, we have an additional implicit reference to Mary's Immaculate Conception taking place before the announcement of the Angel. The Greek word "kekaritomene," is a perfect participle, and so we translate Luke 1:28 most accurately in this way, "Hail, you who have been graced." The Greek translation of the angel's greeting refers to an event of profound grace experienced by Mary that was already completed in the past.[3]

These implicitly revealed seeds of the Immaculate Conception blossomed gradually but steadily in the Tradition of the Church. The early Church Fathers refer to Mary under such titles as "all holy," "all pure," "most innocent," "a miracle of grace," "purer than the angels," "altogether without sin," and these within the first three centuries of the Church. Since the word "immaculate" means "without sin," then the titles used for Mary by the early Fathers, such as "altogether without sin," certainly contain the understanding of her immaculate nature (cf. Pius IX, *Ineffabilis Deus*, 1854).

The early Church Fathers also compared Mary's sinless state as being identical to Eve's state before the participation of Eve in Original Sin. Mary as the "New Eve" was seen to be in the same state of original grace and justice that Eve was in when she was created by God. Since Eve was obviously conceived in grace, without the fallen nature that we receive due to Original Sin, the parallel made by the Church Fathers between Mary and Eve before the fall illustrates their understanding of Mary's likewise immaculate nature.

In the words of St. Ephraem (d.373): "Those two innocent...women, Mary and Eve, had been [created] utterly equal, but afterwards one became the cause of our death, the other the cause of our life." We can see the complete parallel between the sinless Eve before the fall and the sinless Mary. St. Ephraem also refers to Mary's sinless nature in this address to Our Lord: "You and your Mother are the only ones who are immune from all stain; for there is no spot in Thee, O Lord, nor any taint in Your Mother."[4]

In time, references to Mary's Immaculate Conception became more and more explicit and developed. To quote a few examples:

• *St. Ambrose* (d.379) refers to Mary as "free from all stain of sin."[5]

• *St. Severus*, Bishop of Antioch (d.538) states: "She [Mary]...formed part of the human race, and was of the same essence as we, although she was pure from all taint and immaculate."[6]

• *St. Sophronius*, patriarch of Jerusalem (d.638), refers to Mary's pre-purification at conception, addressing the Virgin: "You have found the grace which no one has received.... No one has been pre-purified besides you."[7]

• *St. Andrew of Crete* (d.740) tells us that the Redeemer chose "in all nature this pure and entirely Immaculate Virgin."[8]

• *Theognastes of Constantinople* (c.885) writes: "It was fitting indeed that she who from the beginning had been conceived by a sanctifying action...should also have a holy death...holy, the beginning...holy, the end, holy her whole existence."[9]

These patristic references are important, for occasionally one encounters the misunderstanding that the doctrine of the Immaculate Conception *began* with the infallible declaration of Pius IX in 1854. This position is not only dogmatically confused but is historically in error. These patristic references to the Immaculate Conception within the first five hundreds years and then later within the first millennium of the Church, testify to the growing fundamental understanding of the doctrine present in the Church's Tradition.

Papal Definition of the Immaculate Conception

We see then, how the living Church of Christ grew in its understanding of the divinely revealed truth of Mary's conception without Original Sin. This doctrinal blossoming eventually led to the solemn papal pronouncement of Pius IX in 1854. Let us examine the specific infallible definition of Pius IX.

The papal document *Ineffabilis Deus* in 1854 proclaims as follows:

> We declare, pronounce and define that the doctrine which holds that the Most Blessed Virgin Mary, at the first instant of her conception, was preserved immune from all stain of sin, by a singular grace and privilege of the Omnipotent God, in view of the merits of Jesus Christ, the Savior of the human race, was revealed by God and must be firmly and constantly believed by all the faithful.

We remember that the charism of papal infallibility is that gift of the Holy Spirit which protects the Pope in his office as successor of St. Peter and Vicar of Christ on earth from error regarding a final pronouncement on faith and morals. When speaking *ex cathedra* ("from the chair," or in his official capacity as head of the Church on earth), the Holy Spirit protects the Pope from any error in safeguarding the deposit of faith and morals entrusted to the Church (cf. Mt 16:18; Jn 21:15-17; Lk 22:31).

In this concise *ex cathedra* definition, Pope Pius IX summarizes several foundational elements regarding Mary's Immaculate Conception. First, it states that Mary, from the moment her soul was created and infused into her body (which is known theologically as "passive conception"), was preserved from the effects of Original Sin and, thereby, entered human existence in the state of sanctifying grace.

Due to the sin of our first human parents, all human beings are conceived in a deprived state without the sanctifying grace in their souls that God had originally intended. Hence, there is the need for sacramental Baptism which restores the life of grace in the soul.

Belief in Mary's Immaculate Conception is not difficult, if we remember that it was God's original intention that all humans be conceived in sanctifying grace. God's original plan was for all humans to begin their existence in the family of God in the state of sanctifying grace. It was only as a result of Original Sin that we are now conceived in a state deprived of sanctifying grace. Mary, rather than being the exception, fulfills in a real sense the original intention of what God wanted for all His human children: to be members of His family from the first moment of their existence.

This preservation from Original Sin for Mary was nonetheless "a singular privilege." The definition testifies that the Immaculate Conception was a unique privilege given by the all-powerful God to Mary alone. This free gift from God prepared Mary to be the stainless Mother of God-made-man. And it fittingly allowed Mary to give Jesus an immaculate human nature, identical to her own, which respects the law of motherhood. For we know that God the Son could not be united to a stained fallen nature when he became man. How appropriate it is that Mary could give Jesus an immaculate nature as a mother rightly passes on to her offspring her identical nature.

Mary's Preservative Redemption

An important section of the papal definition states that this unique gift to Mary was granted "in view of the merits of Jesus Christ, the Savior of the human race." Mary received sanctifying grace at conception through an application of the saving graces that Jesus merited for all humanity on the Cross. Mary was redeemed by Jesus Christ as every human being must be.

It was this question of the universal redemption of Jesus Christ that led several noted theologians during the scholastic period of the twelfth and thirteenth centuries to have difficulties[10] in understanding and accepting the Immaculate Conception.

Many theologians viewed Mary's gift of sanctifying grace at conception as running contrary to Scripture passages, like Romans 5, which refer to Christ's need to redeem all humanity because of Original Sin and its effects. It was the insightful contribution of Blessed Duns Scotus (d.1308) who solved this theological misunderstanding with the principle of what is called "Preservative Redemption."

Preservative Redemption explains that Mary's preservation from Original Sin was an application by God of the saving graces merited by Jesus Christ on Calvary. Mary was redeemed at the moment of her conception through sanctifying grace by an application of Jesus' merits on Calvary. God, being out of time, has the power to apply the graces of redemption to individuals in different times of history and did so to Mary at the first moment of her existence.

That Mary's soul was preserved from Original Sin at the moment of conception does not mean that Mary had no need of the redemption of Jesus; rather, Mary owed more to the redemption of Jesus than anyone else. In fact, Mary received from her Son a higher form of redemption.

Why is Mary's Immaculate Conception a higher form of redemption? Because all other human beings are redeemed after they have received a fallen nature through sacramental Baptism. Mary, on the contrary, was redeemed by the grace of Jesus at conception, the grace which prevented Mary from ever receiving a fallen nature. Hence, the grace of Jesus redeemed Mary at conception before her nature was affected by sin. And so, we rightly say that Mary owed more to Christ than anyone else. Through the graces of Jesus at Calvary, Mary never received a fallen nature but was sanctified and thereby redeemed from the first instance of her existence.

This theological contribution by Blessed Duns Scotus helped many a theologian to see the profound complementarity between the universal redemption of Jesus Christ and the Immaculate Conception of His Mother. In short, Mary needed to be saved and was saved in an exalted way by her Son.[11]

The splendor of Mary's Immaculate Conception is echoed in these words of the Second Vatican Council:

> It is no wonder then that it was customary for the Fathers to refer to the Mother of God as all holy and free from every stain of sin, as though fashioned by the Holy Spirit and formed as a new creature. Enriched from the first instant of her conception with the splendor of an entirely unique holiness, the virgin of Nazareth is hailed by the heralding angel, by divine command, as "full of grace" (cf. Lk 1:28)(*Lumen Gentium*, No. 56).

The Virginity of Mary

The third central doctrine regarding the Blessed Virgin is the doctrine of Mary's Perpetual Virginity. This defined truth received unanimous acceptance among the early Church Fathers and was unquestionably confirmed by papal definitions and ecumenical councils alike.

The doctrine of Mary's Perpetual Virginity proclaims that the Blessed Virgin Mary was always a virgin, before, during, and after the birth of Jesus Christ. This threefold character of Mary's physical virginity was stressed in the definition of Pope St. Martin I at the Lateran Synod in 649 A.D. where he declared it an article of faith:

> The blessed ever-virginal and immaculate Mary conceived, without seed, by the Holy Spirit, and without loss of integrity brought Him forth, and after His birth preserved her virginity inviolate.[12]

Let us briefly examine Mary's virginity under these three categories: Mary's virginity before the birth of Christ; her virginity during the birth of Christ; and her virginity following the birth of Christ.

Virginity Before the Birth of Jesus

Mary's virginity before the birth of Jesus is well attested to in Sacred Scripture. The prophecy of Isaiah 7:14 states: "Behold a *virgin* shall conceive...a Son." Likewise in the Gospel of St. Luke, the Angel Gabriel was sent by God "to a virgin...and the virgin's name was Mary" (Lk 1:27). In the dialogue between the Angel Gabriel and Mary we have a further confirmation of Mary's virginity before the birth of Jesus. Gabriel announces:

"You will conceive in your womb and bear a Son" (Lk 1:31). Mary responds: "How will this be since I know not man?" (Lk 1:34). To "know" in this scriptural context is a reference to sexual intercourse. The Angel Gabriel responds: "The Holy Spirit will come upon you and the power of the Most High will overshadow you" (Lk 1:35). The dialogue between Mary and the Angel Gabriel brings out both the virginity of Mary and the conception of Jesus in Mary's womb by the miraculous intervention of the Holy Spirit.

The Apostles' Creed professes the truth of Mary's virginity before the birth of Jesus when it states that Jesus Christ "was conceived by the Holy Spirit, born of the *Virgin* Mary."

The early Fathers of the Church unanimously expressed their belief that Jesus had no human father and was conceived in Mary in a virginal and miraculous manner by the power of the Holy Spirit. This truth was supported by St. Ignatius of Antioch (d.107), St. Justin the Martyr (d.165), St. Irenaeus of Lyon (d.202), and on and on, down the line of the early Church Fathers. Mary's virginity before the birth of Jesus remains a universally accepted Christian truth.

Virginity During the Birth of Jesus

The second aspect of the doctrine refers to Mary's physical virginity during the birth of Our Lord, Jesus Christ. Here we can take a more specific look into what the virginal birth of Jesus truly means.

The papal definition of Mary's continued virginity during the birth of Christ refers to the event that at the appointed time of birth, Jesus left the womb of Mary without loss of Mary's physical virginity. The Church understands Mary's virginity during the birth of Christ as an absence of any physical injury or violation to Mary's virginal seal (in Latin, *virginitas in partu*) through a special divine action of the all-powerful God. This divine act would safeguard Mary's physical virginity which is both symbol and part of her perfect, overall virginity; a virginity both internal and external, of soul and body.

The Fathers of the Church overwhelmingly taught the "miraculous birth" of Jesus that resulted in no injury to Mary's physical integrity. St. Augustine stated: "It is not right that He who came to heal corruption should by His advent violate integrity."[13] Pope St. Leo the Great proclaimed in his famous Tome to Flavian: "Mary brought Him forth, with her virginity untouched, as with her virginity untouched she conceived Him."[14] Later, St. Thomas Aquinas, the Church's greatest theologian, would say of Christ's miraculous birth: "Painlessly,[15] and without change in Mary's virgin body, her Son emerged from the tabernacle of her spotless womb, as He was later to emerge from the tomb, without moving the stone or breaking the seal of Pilate."[16] So as light passes through glass without harming it, so too did Jesus pass through the womb of Mary without the opening of Mary's womb and without any physical harm to the tabernacle of the unborn Christ.[17]

Is there any implicit reference in Sacred Scripture to Mary's virginity during the birth of Christ? Scripture does affirm Mary's virgin birth of Our Lord in the great prophecy of Isaiah 7:14. The prophecy foretells that a virgin, beyond conceiving, will also bear a Son as a virgin: "Behold a *virgin* shall conceive, and bear a son." Therefore, it is not just a virginal conception of Jesus by Mary, but, in fact, a virginal birth as the words "virgin birth" more fully convey.

From the Magisterium, Pope Pius XII in his 1943 encyclical on the Mystical Body of Jesus writes of Mary: "It was she who gave miraculous birth to Christ our Lord" (*Mystici Corporis*).

The Second Vatican Council confirms Mary's virginity both before and during Jesus' birth in these words:

This union of the mother with the Son in the work of salvation is made manifest from the time of Christ's virginal conception...then also at the birth of our Lord, who did not diminish his mother's virginal integrity but sanctified it...(*Lumen Gentium*, No. 57).

Virginity After the Birth of Jesus

Lastly, we examine Mary's virginity after the birth of Jesus. This third aspect of Mary's complete and Perpetual Virginity proclaims that Mary remained a virgin until the end of her earthly life, having no marital relations after Jesus' birth nor having any other children besides Jesus.

This element of the doctrine of Mary's virginity is deeply rooted in Church Tradition and was vigorously defended by the Church Fathers (St. Ephraem, St. Ambrose, St. Augustine, St. Jerome, etc.) whenever early heretical sects denied it. It was explicitly taught by Pope St. Siricius in 392 A.D. The Fifth General Council in 553 A.D. granted Mary the title, "Perpetual Virgin."[18]

Mary is also honored in the liturgy and in many documents of the Magisterium under the title of the "ever virgin Mother of God." The Second Vatican Council continues this Tradition where the Council refers to Mary as the "glorious ever Virgin Mary" (*Lumen Gentium*, No. 52).

An implicit reference to Mary's virginity after birth can be found in Mary's response to the Angel Gabriel: "How will this be since I know not man?" (Lk 1:34). Many Church Fathers understood Mary's response to refer to a vow of perpetual virginity that she had already made and in which she had offered herself as a complete gift to God. Certainly such a vow to God would be continued after the special gift of God to safeguard her virginity both before the birth of Christ and during the birth of

Christ.[19]

Why was it appropriate that Mary should remain virginal after the birth of Our Lord? Clearly, it is in no way intended to infer that marital relations between people in sanctifying grace is not a good and meritorious act. Rather, there are several positive theological reasons why Mary should have remained and did remain virginal after the birth of Christ.

St. Thomas Aquinas explains that Jesus as God was the only-begotten Son of the Father, an only-begotten of such unfathomable dignity as God the Son. So, when Jesus became man, he likewise deserved to be an "only-begotten" Son of His human Mother. The singular nature refers to Christ's special dignity as the God-man. Also, the virginal womb of Mary is the shrine of the Holy Spirit, and a human conception following the miraculous conception by the Holy Spirit would not respect its sacred and unique seed of precedence.

St. Thomas adds that it would be unthinkable that Mary, after her miraculous virginal conception and her miraculous virginal birth, would forfeit her God-protected gift of virginity after the birth of Jesus.[20]

Further, Mary was to be for all ages the perfect example of Christian discipleship in a complete gift of self to God, as well as model of the Church, which is both a virgin and a mother. Mary's virginity would need to be preserved in imitation of the virginity of Jesus Himself, and as perfect example to later Christian disciples of holy virginity as the highest objective gift of self to God.

But Mary's Perpetual Virginity possesses its greatest importance because it safeguards and respects the unprecedented and incomparably sacred event of God becoming man, "born of a woman" (Gal 4:4). Mary, therefore, did not have marital relations or other children to safeguard the uniqueness of the first child and to be the pre-eminent example of Christian discipleship and the model of the Church.

The principal objection to Mary's Perpetual Virginity is the scriptural references to the "brethren of the Lord" (cf. Mt 12:46f, 13:55, Mk 3:31f, etc.). The Greek word for brother, "adelphos," is often used in the Bible to mean cousin, or close relative. There are, in fact, several instances in Sacred Scripture where "adelphos" is used, and in the context it cannot mean blood brother (for example, the relationship between Lot and Abraham [Gen 13:8], and the relationship between Jacob and Laban [Gen 29:15]).

The term "brethren" of Jesus in the New Testament would thereby refer to His cousins, His near relatives, and possibly His close followers or His disciples, as Christians today still refer to each other as "brothers and sisters" in the Lord.

This and other objections to Mary's Perpetual Virginity will be more fully discussed in Chapter 7, "In Defense of Mary."

The Assumption of Mary

The fourth central Marian doctrine is the Assumption of Mary. The doctrine of Mary's Assumption, like her Immaculate Conception, has the added certainty of an infallible papal statement. Pope Pius XII in 1950 defined the Assumption of Mary in the following statement: "The Immaculate Mother of God, the ever Virgin Mary, having completed the course of her earthly life, was assumed body and soul into heavenly glory" (*Munificentissimus Deus*).

What evidence is present in the sources of Divine Revelation for the doctrine of Mary's glorious Assumption? Pope Pius XII, in his papal document, declares the Assumption a doctrine "revealed by God" and refers to several sources.

The Magisterium of the Church

The doctrine of Mary's Assumption received the unanimous consensus from the Magisterium of the Church. In 1946, Pope Pius XII petitioned the bishops of the world asking them whether the Assumption of Mary could be defined and whether they favored such a definition. Out of 1232 bishops, 1210 enthusiastically answered yes to both questions (over ninety-eight percent). Such near unanimity among the bishops of the Church is almost unprecedented in the history of the Church regarding doctrinal pronouncements.

Pope Pius XII, therefore, in the service of the bishops and of the common faithful, used the charism of infallibility to define and confirm this universally accepted doctrine. In fact, after the papal definition of the Immaculate Conception in 1854, the Vatican received millions of petitions from bishops, priests, religious, and faithful alike asking for the definition of the Assumption of Mary.

The Assumption in Scripture

A seed of the doctrine of Mary's Assumption is found in Sacred Scripture, in Genesis 3:15. As the papal document of Pius XII explains, Genesis 3:15 foreshadows Mary as intimately sharing in the same absolute victory of her Son over Satan: "I will put enmity between you and the woman, and between your seed and her seed..." (Gen 3:15).

According to St. Paul (cf. Rom 5-8; Hebrews 2), the consequences of Satan's seed, evil, are twofold: sin and death (or bodily corruption). Therefore, Mary, who shared in her Son's victory over Satan and his seed, would have to be saved from both sin and death or corruption.

Mary did triumph over sin in her Immaculate Conception

and triumphed over death (specifically corruption of the body) in her glorious Assumption at the end of her earthly life.

It is worthy of note that many bishops from around the world sent to Pius XII the same scriptural support from Genesis 3:15 for Mary's Assumption. So there had been some general episcopal confirmation that Genesis 3:15 is the primary doctrinal seed in Scripture for Mary's Assumption.[21] Other scriptural support for the Assumption of Mary includes Lk 1:28, since her bodily assumption is a natural effect of being "full of grace"; Revelation 12:1, where Mary's coronation implies her preceding bodily assumption; 1 Corinthians 15:23 and Matthew 27:52-53 which support the possibility of a bodily assumption: "Arise, O Lord, into your resting place: you and the ark which you have sanctified" (Ps 131:8).

The Assumption in Tradition

The doctrine of Mary's Assumption is also found in Sacred Tradition. The early Christians gradually unraveled the implicitly revealed reference to Mary's Assumption. Our first explicit reference is by St. Gregory of Tours (d.593): "The Lord commanded the holy body [of Mary] to be borne on a cloud to Paradise where, reunited to its soul and exalting with the elect, it enjoys the everlasting bliss of eternity."[22]

From the seventh century onwards, numerous Church Fathers proclaimed the doctrine of the Assumption (St. Germain of Constantinople, d.733; St. Andrew of Crete d.740; St. John Damascene, d.749, etc.). During the sixth century, the first liturgical feasts dedicated to the Assumption appear in Syria and in the Alexandrian church in Egypt. Western liturgical feasts dedicated to Mary's Assumption take place in Gaul (modern day France) in the seventh century; and by the eighth century it was celebrated in Rome. From the thirteenth century on, the doctrine of Mary's Assumption was taught with near unanimity by Church writers and theologians in both the East and West.[23]

Relation to Other Marian Doctrines

Pius XII makes a major point for the validity of Mary's Assumption as a definable doctrine by drawing an *essential* connection between the Assumption and other Marian-defined doctrines, in particular, the motherhood of God and the Immaculate Conception.

As for the connection between the Assumption of Mary and her motherhood of God, Pope Pius XII states that it is fitting that Jesus would honor His Mother as only a divine Son could. No one obeys the fourth commandment of honoring father and mother better than Jesus, who is Son of the Father and Son of Mary. It is thereby reasonable that Jesus would uniquely honor His Mother, first, by preserving her from the corruption of the grave, and secondly, by granting her a glorification of the body in Heaven before the general resurrection of the body for all other saints on the last day.[24]

Even more evident is the Assumption in its essential connection to Mary's Immaculate Conception. Simply put, Mary's Assumption is the natural effect of her Immaculate Conception. The Assumption is the logical effect of being preserved from Original Sin, since corruption of the body is an effect of Original Sin (cf. Rom 5-8; Heb 2). Had Adam and Eve not sinned, they, too, at the end of their earthly life could have been assumed into Heaven without the corruption of their bodies. Corruption of the body is a result of Original Sin. Therefore, since Mary was preserved from Original Sin in her Immaculate Conception, and since she sustained her fullness of grace given by God, Our Lady could not have experienced the fruit of Original Sin in the corruption of the body at the end of her earthly life.

The doctrines of the Immaculate Conception and the Assumption are interiorly and logically connected, as Pius XII explains in the papal document:

These two privileges (i.e., the Assumption and the Immaculate Conception) are most closely bound to one another. Indeed, Christ overcame sin and death by His own death, and the man who, through baptism, is supernaturally regenerated, has conquered sin and death through the same Christ. However, as a general rule, God does not wish to grant to the just the full effect of their victory over death until the end of time shall have come. And so it is that the bodies of even the just are corrupted after death, and that only on the last day will they be joined, each to his own glorified soul. Nevertheless, God has willed that the Blessed Virgin Mary should be exempted from this general law. By an entirely unique privilege she completely overcame sin through her Immaculate Conception, and therefore was not subject to that law of remaining in the corruption of the grave, nor did she have to wait until the end of time for the redemption of her body (*Munificentissimus Deus*, No. 4, 5).

The question may then be asked: Did Mary die? Human death may be defined as a separation of soul and body at the end of earthly life. The Church has never defined whether or not at the end of Mary's earthly life she experienced some temporary separation of soul and body before her Assumption into Heaven. Such a temporary separation of soul and body, as long as it did not include any material corruption of the body (the effect of sin), could have been experienced by the Mother of Jesus. Pius XII purposely avoided any direct statement regarding Mary's death by using the more general expression "at the end of her earthly life." The majority of theologians hold that Mary did experience some type of temporary death so as to enter Heaven in the manner which most closely resembled that of her Son. What is certain is that Mary could not experience the *corruption of the body*, the "material death" that comes as a result of Original Sin.

The words of Vatican II well attest to the unique event of Mary's glorious Assumption as a proper earthly end to the one who, in all her doctrines, reflects a person of perfect obedience to God's will and of intimate and singular union with her Son, Our Lord:

> Finally the Immaculate Virgin preserved from all stain of original sin, was taken up body and soul into heavenly glory, when her earthly life was over, and exalted by the Lord as Queen over all things, that she might be the more fully conformed to her Son, the Lord of lords (cf. Apoc 19:16) and conqueror of sin and death (*Lumen Gentium*, No. 59).

These four central doctrines of the Blessed Virgin, her Divine Motherhood, Immaculate Conception, Perpetual Virginity and Assumption, reveal the unique role of the Virgin of Nazareth in God's perfect plan of salvation. We will see a profound complementarity and convergence of these doctrines and their concurring Marian privileges as we examine Mary's fifth doctrinal role as Spiritual Mother of Christ's faithful and as Co-redemptrix and Mediatrix of Graces.

Surely in light of the sublime graces and privileges poured upon the Virgin and manifested in these doctrines, there was more than ample reason for the Marian self-prophecy that "all generations will call me blessed" (Lk 1:48).

Notes

1. Cf. Gerald van Ackeren, S.J., "Mary's Divine Motherhood" in *Mariology*, Vol. II, 1957. Juniper Carol, O.F.M., *Fundamentals of Mariology*, New York, Benzinger Bros., 1957, p. 35-40.

2. Although some translations have the pronoun "she" for the one crushing the serpent's head, the original Hebrew somewhat favors the masculine "he." But in either case, the victory over Satan is ultimately that of Jesus Christ with Mary's instrumental participation as the "New Eve."

3. Cf. Carol, *Fundamentals*, p. 90.

4. St. Ephraem, *Sermones exegetici, opera omnia syriace et latine*, 2 (Rome, 1740), 327.

5. St. Ambrose, *Exposito in Psalm 118*, Sermon 22, n. 30, PL 15, 1599.

6. St. Severus, *Hom. cathedralis*, 67, PO 8, 350.

7. St. Sophronius, *Orat in Deiparae Annunt.*, 25, PG 87, 3246-3247.

8. St. Andrew, *Hom. 1 in Nativ. Deiparae*, PG 97, 913-914.

9. Theognostes, *Hom. in Dorm. Deiparae*, Patrologia Orientalis (PO) Greffin-Nau, 16, 467.

10. The other principal objection to the Immaculate Conception in the scholastic age was based on the misunderstood notion of how Original Sin was transmitted. Since they erroneously held that Original Sin was transmitted from an infected body to the soul once the soul was created and infused, then Mary would have contracted Original Sin from the fallen nature of St. Anne, her mother. It was Blessed Duns Scotus who correctly clarified that Original Sin consisted rather in the absence of sanctifying grace in the soul at conception, a deprivation caused by the sin of Adam and Eve. Hence, Mary, by the merits of Jesus Christ, was granted that gift of sanctifying grace in her soul at conception.

11. Cf. Burghart, S.J., "Mary in Eastern Patristic Thought" in *Mariology*, Vol. II; Carr, "Mary's Immaculate Conception" in *Mariology*, Vol. I; O'Carroll, "Immaculate Conception" in *Theotokos*; Carol, *Fundamentals*, p. 90-115.

12. Denzinger's *Enchiridion Symbolorum* (DS), 256.

13. St. Augustine, *Serm.* 189, n.2; PL 38, 1005.

14. Pope St. Leo, *Enchiridion Patristicum* (EP) 2182.

15. Furthermore, it follows that Mary's birth of Jesus would be a painless experience, since pain in childbirth is a punitive effect of Original Sin (cf. Gen 3:15). Mary, being free from the penalty of Original Sin due to her Immaculate Conception, would likewise be free from the penalty of a painful process of childbirth.

16. St. Thomas Aquinas, *Summa Theologica*, III, Q. 28, a. 2.

17. Cf. Carol, *Fundamentals*, p. 147; Carol, "Mary's Virginity in Partu," *Homiletic and Pastoral Review*, 54, 1954.

18. DS 214; cf. Burghart, "Mary in Eastern Patristic Thought," *Mariology*, Vol. II.

19. Cf. Collins, S.J., "Our Lady's Vow of Virginity" in *Catholic Biblical Quarterly*, 5, 1943.

20. St. Thomas Aquinas, *Summa Theologica* III, Q 28, a. 3.

21. Cf. Carol, *Fundamentals*, pp. 185.
22. St. Gregory of Tours, *Libri miraculorum*, lib I, cap. 4; PL 71, 708.
23. Cf. Carol, *Fundamentals*, p. 188.
24. Cf. Pius XII, *Munificentissimus Deus*, 1950.

chapter three

Mary, Spiritual Mother and Mediatrix

What do all the doctrines that God has revealed about the Blessed Virgin have to do with me personally? How do these revealed truths about the Mother of Jesus affect my own spiritual life?

It is in answer to these questions and to others that we now explore Mary's God-given role as Spiritual Mother of humanity and as Co-redemptrix and Mediatrix. For it is by understanding Mary as Spiritual Mother in its fullness that allows for the foundation of an authentic Catholic response to Mary.

By an authentic Catholic response we mean here a response both "from the head" and "from the heart"; both theologically and spiritually; in a phrase, our personal and ecclesial response to Mary. So Mary's role as Spiritual Mother and Mediatrix can rightly be called the bridge between authentic Marian doctrine and devotion.

First, we will look at the basic understanding of the spiritual motherhood of Mary and then continue to its fullest and most profound understanding in the role of the Mother of Jesus as Co-redemptrix and Mediatrix of all graces.

Spiritual Motherhood

Along with Mary's yes to being the Mother of the Savior at the Annunciation (Lk 1:26f), the principal scriptural basis for the doctrine of Mary as Spiritual Mother of all humanity is found in John 19:26-27. Here Mary is on Calvary at the foot of the Cross with her crucified Son and John, the beloved disciple. As the Gospel of John reads: "When Jesus saw his mother, and the disciple whom he loved standing near, he said to his mother, 'Woman, behold your son.' Then he said to the disciple, 'Behold your mother'" (Jn 19:26-27).

John, the "beloved disciple," is a symbol of all humanity and, in a special way, of every person who likewise seeks to be a "beloved disciple" of Jesus. That John is symbolic of all humanity and, in a special way, of all the faithful, has been confirmed by several popes, not to mention an endless list of theologians and spiritual writers. For example, Pope Leo XIII writes: "Now in John, according to the constant mind of the Church, Christ designated the whole human race, particularly those who were joined with him in faith" (*Adjutricem populi*).

More recently, Pope John Paul II discusses Mary's motherhood as a personal gift which Christ gives to John, and beyond John to every individual:

The Mother of Christ, who stands at the very center of this mystery—a mystery which embraces each individual and all humanity—is given as mother to every single individual and all humanity. The man at the foot of the Cross is John, "the disciple whom he [Jesus] loved." But it is not he alone. Following tradition, the Council [Vatican II] does not hesitate to call Mary *the Mother of Christ and mother of mankind....*" "Indeed she is 'clearly the mother of the members of Christ...since she cooperated out of love so that there might be born in the

Church the faithful.'" ...Mary's motherhood, which became man's inheritance, is a gift: *a gift which Christ himself makes* personally to every individual (*Redemptoris Mater*, No. 23,45).

Note that the words of Christ, rather than proposing a suggestion, state a theological fact. Our Lord says: "Behold, your mother." He does not passively invite us to accept Mary as Mother; rather, He states the theological fact that Mary is the newly God-given Mother of each beloved disciple. Our remaining question then should not so much be, "Is Mary our Mother?" but more appropriately, "How do we properly implement the words of Christ to 'behold our mother'?"

Spiritual Motherhood in Tradition

The Fathers of the Church recognized Mary's role as Spiritual Mother as it was essentially contained in her example and role as the "New Eve." Mary was the new "mother of the living" who participated with Jesus, the New Adam, in regaining the life of grace for the human family. Since the name "Eve" means "mother of the living," then Mary, as the New Eve, is the "new mother of the living" in the order of grace. Again, as St. Jerome summed it up, "Death through Eve, life through Mary."

Further, the prayers of petition offered in the early Church to the Mother of God for spiritual and physical protection manifest an understanding of Mary's ability to intercede for her spiritual children. We see this son- or daughter-like petition for the special aid of our Spiritual Mother in the *Sub Tuum*: "We fly to your patronage, O holy Mother of God. Despise not our petitions in our necessities, but deliver us from all dangers, O ever glorious and blessed Virgin."

St. Augustine saw Mary's spiritual maternity based on the

mystical union between Christ and the faithful. As physical Mother of Christ, the Head, Mary in a spiritual manner is Mother also of the faithful that make up the Body of Christ.[1]

The voice of the Magisterium has been clear and consistent regarding the doctrine of Mary's spiritual motherhood. The first Pope to refer to Mary as Spiritual Mother, particularly as "Mother of Grace," was Pope Sixtus IV in 1477 (Apostolic Constitution *Cum praecelsa*). Since Pope Sixtus IV, no less than twenty-seven subsequent popes have declared Mary as Spiritual Mother with an always increasing specificity and clarity.[2]

Vatican II granted the confirmation of an ecumenical council to the doctrine of Mary's spiritual motherhood when it declared: "Thus, in a wholly singular way she cooperated by her obedience, faith, hope and burning charity in the work of the Savior in restoring supernatural life to souls. For this reason she is a mother to us in the order of grace" (*Lumen Gentium*, No.61).

Theology of Mary as Spiritual Mother

But how do we explain theologically Mary's role as Spiritual Mother? Her spiritual motherhood is intimately related to the doctrine of the Mystical Body of Jesus Christ. In the rich doctrine of the Mystical Body according to St. Paul (cf. Col 1:18, Eph 4:15), Christ is the Head of the Body, and the Church is the Body of Christ. Mary, then, in conceiving Jesus, the Head of the Mystical Body, also conceived all the faithful since we all are members of that same Body. In giving birth to Jesus the Head, Mary also gives birth to the Body, the Church. So, Mary, in giving physical birth to Jesus, made it possible for His members to receive spiritual life through Jesus. It is for this reason that Mary is called our true "Spiritual Mother."

She is not our physical Mother, nor is the title a mere figure of speech. Mary, in giving birth to Jesus, truly communicated to us the supernatural life of grace that allows us to become children of God. This is why Mary, during medieval times, was referred to as the "Neck of the Mystical Body." It is she who connects the Head with the members of the Body in the order of grace. And since the Head should never be separated from the Body, it is Mary that is Mother to both: Mother to Jesus the Head, physically; and Mother to the members of the Mystical Body, spiritually. As explained by Pope St. Pius X in his famous Marian encyclical:

> Is not Mary the Mother of Christ? She is therefore our Mother also.... He [Jesus] acquired a body composed like that of other men, but as Savior of our race, He had a kind of spiritual and mystical body, which is the society of those who believe in Christ.... Consequently, Mary, bearing in her own womb the Savior, may be said to have borne also those whose life was contained in the life of the Savior. All of us, therefore...have come forth from the womb of Mary as a body united to its head. Hence, in a spiritual and mystical sense, we are called children of Mary, and she is the Mother of us all (*Ad diem illum Laetissimum*).

But Mary's spiritual motherhood to us in grace does not stop only at the birth of the Mystical Body. A true mother both "natures" and "nurtures" her children. A true mother gives birth to her children, and she also nourishes and forms her children. Spiritually, then, Mary not only gave birth to the Body of Christ, but also continually intercedes in obtaining graces for her spiritual children, leading them to her Son and to eternal salvation. Mary does so, not only in virtue of conceiving the Mystical Body of Jesus at the Annunciation (Lk 1:26), but also by sharing in the sufferings of her crucified Son on Calvary (Jn 19:26) where she is definitively given as Spiritual Mother to all beloved disciples and to humanity in general.

Hence, Mary became our Spiritual Mother initially at the Annunciation, but her motherhood was perfected on Calvary, participating in the spiritual regeneration or rebirth of the human family. The exercise of her motherhood continues in her constant intercession from Heaven in leading her earthly children to their heavenly home.

As the Second Vatican Council profoundly summarizes:

> This motherhood of Mary in the order of grace continues uninterruptedly from the consent which she loyally gave at the Annunciation and which she sustained without wavering beneath the cross until the eternal fulfilment of all the elect. Taken up to heaven she did not lay aside this saving office but by her manifold intercession continues to bring us the gifts of eternal salvation. By her maternal charity, she cares for the brethren of her Son, who still journey on earth surrounded by dangers and difficulties, until they are led into their blessed home (*Lumen Gentium*, No. 62).

This is the sound theological basis that led Pope Paul VI during the Second Vatican Council to proclaim Mary as "Mother of the Church." For Mary is the Christ-designated Spiritual Mother of the members of the Mystical Body of Jesus, which is the Church.

Queenship of Mary

Another dimension of Mary's spiritual motherhood is the Queenship of Mary. Queenship can be understood in one of two ways. A queen can be a "female king" or independent ruler of a kingdom, or she can be the mother or spouse of the king. It is only in the second relative sense that Mary is rightly understood as Queen, as true Mother of Christ the "King," whose kingdom is the Mystical Body.

Mary is thereby Queen in the Kingdom of God. As Mother of Christ the King, she intercedes for the members of the Kingdom of God. This "Queen Mother" guides and rules the members of her Son's kingdom in complete subordination and submission to Christ the King in the law and order of sanctifying grace.

Mary's Queenship is referred to in Revelation 12:1, where Mary is portrayed with the moon under her feet and wearing a crown of twelve stars, and as Mother of her Son, the King who will rule all nations, she is taken up to His throne (Rev 12:5).

Maternal Mediatrix

A mediator, in general, is a person who intervenes between two other persons for the goal of uniting the two parties. The task of the mediator is not to distance further but to reconcile, to bring together the two parties in question.

In the Christian faith, we know that there is only one unique mediator between God and man: the person of Jesus Christ. As St. Paul says: "For there is one God and there is one mediator between God and men, the man Christ Jesus" (1 Tim 2:5). But the perfect mediation of Jesus Christ does not prevent (and in fact provides for) other mediators who are subordinate and secondary to Jesus. Jesus' perfect mediation allows for others to *participate* in the one and unique mediation of Our Lord.

We have several examples of secondary mediators in the Old Testament, mediators that were appointed by Almighty God Himself. We have the Old Testament prophets who are inspired by God to mediate between Yahweh and the oftentimes disobedient people of Israel (for the purpose of reconciling Yahweh and

Israel). Certainly the patriarchs, like Abraham and Moses, were secondary mediators of the covenant between God and the chosen people of the Old Testament.

In both Old and New Testaments, the glorious mediation of the angels fills the pages of Sacred Scripture as God's special messengers and intercessors; for example, from the Book of Tobit, to the mediation of the Angel Gabriel on behalf of God at the Annunciation (cf. Lk 1:26). St. Thomas Aquinas called the angels "God's secondary causes" since God does so much through the mediation of the angels.

That the one mediation of Jesus Christ is unique, but at the same time allows for the subordinate and secondary mediation of others, is here summarized by St. Thomas Aquinas: "Christ alone is the perfect mediator between God and man...but there is nothing to prevent others in a certain way from being called mediators between God and man in so far as they, by preparing or serving, cooperate in uniting men to God." [3]

Vatican II voices the same truth in these words:

> No creature could ever be counted along with the Incarnate Word and Redeemer; but just as the priesthood of Christ is shared in various ways both by his ministers and the faithful, and as the one goodness of God is radiated in different ways among his creatures, so also the unique mediation of the Redeemer does not exclude but rather gives rise to a manifold cooperation which is but a sharing in this one source (*Lumen Gentium*, No. 62).

Hence, even we, in offering a prayer or fasting for a family member or friend, are acting as secondary mediators between God and humanity in the order of spiritual intercession which, rather than detracting from the one mediation of Jesus, in fact, manifests and exercises the power of our one Divine Mediator to the Father.

Theologically, in regards to Mary, the term "mediatrix" refers to a secondary and subordinate female mediator who acts with the same intention as the primary and independent mediator; that is, the reconciliation of individuals. Mary participates in the one mediation of Jesus Christ like no other creature, and hence, she exclusively has the role of "Mediatrix" with Jesus in reconciling humanity with God.

Several scriptural events point to Mary's role as Mediatrix in the order of intercession. It was Mary's intercession at the wedding of Cana (Jn 2) that led to the first miracle of Our Lord and the beginning of His public ministry. At the Visitation of Mary to Elizabeth, Mary's physical intercession in bringing the unborn Christ to His unborn cousin, John the Baptist, led to John's sanctification in the womb of Elizabeth (cf. Lk 1:41).

This role of Mary as "Mediatrix," or secondary and subordinate mediator, with Jesus has a strong foundation in the apostolic tradition as manifested in this fourth century profession by St. Ephraem (d. 373): "After the Mediator, you [Mary] are the Mediatrix of the whole world."[4]

More recently, Vatican II ends its beautiful treatment of Mary as "Mother in the order of grace" by confirming Mary's role and title as "Mediatrix":

> Therefore the Blessed Virgin is invoked in the Church under the titles of Advocate, Helper, Benefactress, and Mediatrix. This, however, is so understood that it neither takes away anything from nor adds anything to the dignity and efficacy of Christ the one Mediator (*Lumen Gentium*, No. 62.).

Pope John Paul II explains Mary's unique and exalted sharing in the one mediation of Jesus in his 1987 encyclical, "Mother of the Redeemer":

Mary *entered, in a way all her own, into the one mediation* "between God and men" *which is the mediation of the man Christ Jesus* [1 Tim 2:5]. [W]e must say that through this fullness of grace and supernatural life she was especially predisposed to cooperation with Christ, the one Mediator of human salvation. *And such cooperation is precisely this mediation subordinated* to the mediation of Christ. In Mary's case we have a special and exceptional mediation...(*Redemptoris Mater*, No. 39).

Mary's role as Mediatrix with Jesus, the one Mediator, has two fundamental expressions in the order of grace. First, Mary uniquely participated with Jesus Christ in reconciling God and man through the Redemption. For this role she has been called "Co-redemptrix" (meaning a secondary and subordinate participator in Jesus' Redemption of the world).

Secondly, Mary gave birth to Jesus, source of all grace, and she distributes the graces merited by Jesus on Calvary to the human family. This role of Mary as the person responsible for the distribution of graces is referred to as "Dispenser of all graces" or oftentimes by the more general title, "Mediatrix of all graces." Because of the importance of both of these two elements of Mary's role as Mediatrix, let us examine them individually.

Co-redemptrix

When the Church calls Mary the "Co-redemptrix," she means that Mary uniquely participated in the Redemption of humanity with her Son Jesus Christ, although in a completely subordinate and dependent manner to that of her Son. Mary participated in Jesus' reconciliation of the human family with God like no other created person. Mary's unique participation in the Redemption was scripturally foreshadowed in the prophecy of Simeon at the Temple where he said to Mary: "a sword will pierce your own heart, too" (Lk 2:35).

How did the Mother of Jesus do this? First of all, Mary participated in Redemption by accepting the invitation of the angel to become the Mother of God and by giving flesh to the Savior. Early Church Fathers saw the Incarnation and Redemption as one, unified, saving act (since the Angel Gabriel outlined Jesus' redemptive act in his heavenly message), and Mary brought the world its Redeemer at the Incarnation.

The parallel between Eve and Mary is significant here. As Eve gave the fruit to Adam as the instrument for the fall of humanity, Mary gave the body to Jesus as the instrument for the Redemption of humanity. As Hebrews 10:10 tells us, the *body* of Jesus Christ was the instrument for the Redemption of the human family. Since the very instrument for the Redemption, the body of Jesus, was given to Him by Mary, the Mother of Jesus clearly played an intimate part in the redeeming of the human race with her Son, far beyond that of any other creature.

Secondly, Mary uniquely participated in the sacrifice of Jesus on Calvary for the Redemption of humanity (theologically referred to as "objective redemption"). Mary offered the maternal rights of her Son on the cross to the Father in perfect obedience to God's will, and in atonement for the sins of the world. Mary's offering of her own Son on Calvary, along with her own motherly compassion, rights, and suffering, offered in union with her Son for the salvation of the human family, merited more graces than any other created person.[5] As Pope Pius XII confirmed in his encyclical *On the Mystical Body*, Mary "offered Him on Golgotha to the Eternal Father, together with the holocaust of her maternal rights and her motherly love, like a New Eve for all children of Adam" (*Mystici Corporis*).

Mary, in an act of obedience to the will of God, offered Jesus, and with Jesus, her own suffering by sharing in the experience of the passion and death of Our Lord in atonement for our sins. It is in this sense that we say Mary offered her maternal rights on Calvary and rightly refer to Mary as the Co-redemptrix with the Redeemer.

Again it must be stated that Mary's participation in the redemption of the human family was completely and in every way secondary and dependent to the sacrifice of Jesus the Savior. Hence, the title Co-redemptrix should never be interpreted as Mary having an equal role in the salvation of the world with Jesus. At the same time, her truly meritorious act of giving flesh to the Redeemer and of participating uniquely in Jesus' painful sacrifice rightly won for her the title of Co-redemptrix.

Papal Teaching

The Church's Magisterium has unquestionably confirmed the completely subordinate but authentic co-redeeming role of the Mother of Jesus. Let us cite a few papal examples:

• *Pope Benedict XV* in his 1918 apostolic letter stated: "To such extent did she [Mary] suffer and almost die with her suffering and dying Son, and to such extent did she surrender her maternal rights over her Son for man's salvation...that we may rightly say that she together with Christ redeemed the human race" (Inter Sodalicia).

• *Pope Pius XI* (1922-1939) referred to Mary as the Co-redemptrix no less than six times in various papal documents. In one papal statement Pope Pius addressed Mary in these words, "O Mother of piety and mercy who, when thy most beloved Son was accomplishing the Redemption of the human race on the altar of the cross, did stand there both suffering with Him, and as a Co-redemptrix; preserve in us the precious fruit of this Redemption and of thy compassion."[6]

• *Pope Pius XII* (1939-1958) used the title "Loving Associate of the Redeemer" to describe Mary's unique participation in Redemption[7] and gave the following explanation:

> By the willing of God, the most Blessed Virgin Mary was inseparably joined with Christ in accomplishing the work of man's Redemption, so that our salvation flows from the love of Jesus Christ and his sufferings intimately united with the love and sorrows of his mother (*Haurietis Aguas*, No. 2).

• *The Second Vatican Council* beautifully synthesized Mary's unique participation in the Redemption with the following words:

> Thus the Blessed Virgin advanced in her pilgrimage of faith, and faithfully persevered in her union with her Son unto the cross, where she stood, in keeping with the divine plan, enduring with her only begotten Son the intensity of his suffering, associated herself with his sacrifice in her mother's heart, and lovingly consenting to the immolation of this victim which was born of her (*Lumen Gentium*, No. 58).

• *John Paul II* in his 1987 Marian encyclical continued the papal affirmation of Mary's unique participation in Redemption, calling it "perhaps the deepest 'kenosis' of faith in human history":

> How great, how heroic then is the *obedience of faith* shown by Mary in the face of God's "unsearchable judgments"! How completely she "abandons herself to God" without reserve, "offering the full consent of the intellect and will" to him whose "ways are inscrutable" (cf. Rom 11:33)! *[T]hrough this faith Mary is perfectly*

united with Christ in his self-emptying....At the foot of the Cross Mary shares through faith in the shocking mystery of this self-emptying. This is perhaps the deepest *"kenosis" of faith* in human history. Through faith the Mother shares in the death of her Son, in his redeeming death...(*Redemptoris Mater*, No. 18).

• And in a 1985 papal statement, John Paul specifically used the title Co-redemptrix in developing the understanding of Mary's *spiritual crucifixion* at the foot of the cross:

Crucified spiritually with her crucified Son (cf. Gal 2:20), she contemplated with heroic love the death of her God, she "lovingly consented to the immolation of this Victim which she herself had brought forth" (*Lumen Gentium*, No. 58)...as she was in a special way close to the Cross of her Son, she also had to have a privileged experience of his Resurrection. In fact, Mary's role as *co-redemptrix* did not cease with the glorification of her Son.[8]

Mediatrix of All Graces

Mary's role as dispenser or mediatrix of the graces of the Redemption follows appropriately from her role as Co-redemptrix. It is important to see that Our Lady dispenses the graces of Jesus because of her special participation in meriting the graces of Redemption.

Mary uniquely participated in the Redemption of humanity by Jesus Christ and; therefore, the Mother of Jesus, above all creatures, fittingly participates in the distribution of these graces to the members of the Mystical Body (theologically called "subjective redemption"). By distributing sanctifying grace,

Mary is able to fulfill her role as Spiritual Mother, since she spiritually nourishes the faithful of Christ's body in the order of grace. Mary's God-given ability to distribute the graces of Redemption by her intercession is an essential element and full flowering of her role as Spiritual Mother. For true motherhood goes beyond the birthing of children to include their nourishing, growth, and proper formation.

In sum, the Mother of Jesus mediates all the graces of Jesus to the human family in two regards. First, Mary mediated all graces to humanity by giving birth to Jesus and by bringing the source and author of all graces to the world [cf. Lk 2:6-7] (theologically called "remote mediation"). Secondly, Mary mediates all graces by distributing the graces merited on Calvary to the human family by her willed intercession [cf. Jn 19:26] (theologically called "proximate" or "immediate" mediation).

Notice the divine consistency in Mary's role in the order of grace as designated by God's perfect will. First of all, Mary is conceived in sanctifying grace from the first instant of her existence by a unique act of God's perfect will. Then Mary gives birth to the source of all graces in Jesus Christ. With this birth of the Head of Grace, she also gives spiritual birth to the Body mystically united with the Head in grace. Furthermore, she participates with her Son in meriting grace that redeems the world on Calvary. Finally, from Heaven, Mary distributes the graces of the Redemption to grant to each open heart of the human family the saving supernatural life of Our Lord. As Vatican II ascribes to her, Mary is truly our Mother in the order of grace.

When the Church says that the Mother of Jesus is Mediatrix of all graces, she means that all favors and graces granted by God to humanity reach us through the intercession of Mary. To receive all graces through Mary is simply to continue the perfect plan of God which began with His gift of the source of all graces, Jesus Christ, who came to us through Mary. The Mother of

Jesus, subordinate and perfectly conformed to the will of her Son, distributes the graces of Redemption to the human family by her willed intercession (theologically referred to as "secondary moral cause").

Does this mean that the graces of Jesus will not be distributed unless we pray directly to the Blessed Virgin? No. But it does express the truth that whether we call directly upon the name of Mary or not, we, nonetheless, receive all graces through her actual and personally willed intercession.

This is analogous to the authentic Catholic understanding of Baptism of desire. A person who is not Christian can attain eternal life under specific conditions of charity and contrition through Jesus, the one Redeemer and Mediator to the Father, without knowing during his earthly life that it is through the mediation of Jesus. In a similar way, all who receive the graces of Jesus Christ do so through Mary, even if they lack knowledge of Mary's intercession. Theologically, this is the difference between knowledge and causality.

At the same time, we must remember how pleasing it is to God when the human family does affirm His manifest will by directly invoking His appointed distributor of graces by name. It is our human way of saying yes to God's order of things, which includes Mary as the distributor of graces.

Papal Teaching on Mediatrix of All Graces

The unanimous voices of the popes of the last two centuries on this pivotal Marian doctrine of Mediatrix of all graces manifest nothing short of incontestable consistency and certainty regarding the revealed truth of this doctrine. Let us look at some of the more important papal pronouncements and explanations on this doctrine. Several of these papal statements provide profound, theological explanations as to why Mary is the fitting distributor of all graces.

• *Pope Pius VII* (1800-1823) referred to Mary as the "Dispensatrix of all graces."[9]

• *Pope Pius IX* (1846-1878), the Marian pope who defined Mary's Immaculate Conception, wrote: "...God has committed to Mary the treasury of all good things, in order that everyone may know that through her are obtained every hope, every grace, and all salvation" (*Ubi primum*).

• *Pope Leo XIII* (1878-1903) frequently referred to Mary's role as "Dispenser of all heavenly graces" and boldly professed these words about Mary's role as Mediatrix of all graces:

> With equal truth can it be affirmed that, by the will of God, *nothing* of the immense treasure of every grace which the Lord has accumulated, comes to us except through Mary.... How great are the wisdom and mercy revealed in this design of God.... Mary is our glorious intermediary; she is the powerful Mother of the omnipotent God.... This design of such dear mercy realized by God in Mary and confirmed by the testament of Christ (Jn 19:26-27) was understood from the beginning and accepted with the utmost joy by the holy Apostles and earliest believers. It was also the belief and teachings of the venerable Fathers of the Church. All the Christian peoples of every age accepted it unanimously.... There is no other reason for this than divine faith (*Octobri mense*).

This papal proclamation of Leo XIII not only proposed the truth that all graces of God come to us through Mary, but also that this belief has been the universal belief of the Church from the apostolic days to our present day. This reality, he said, can only be explained through God's revelation in "divine faith."

• *Pope St. Pius X* (1903-1914) continued the remarkable

papal consistency by calling Mary "the dispenser of all gifts," and he discusses theologically how Jesus is the source of all graces, and Mary is the channel of all graces:

> By this union of will and suffering between Christ and Mary, "she merited to become in a most worthy manner the Reparatrix of the lost world" and consequently, the Dispensatrix of all gifts which Jesus acquired for us through His death and blood. Indeed, we do not deny that the distribution of these gifts belongs by strict and proper right to Christ.... Yet...it was granted to the august Virgin to be together with her only-begotten Son the most powerful Mediatrix and conciliatrix of the whole world. So Christ is the source...Mary, however, as St. Bernard justly remarks, is the channel, or she is the neck by which the Body is united to the Head and the Head sends power and strength through the Body. For she is the neck of our Head, through which all spiritual gifts are communicated to His Body (*Ad diem illum Laetissimum*).

• *Pope Benedict XV* (1914-1922) strongly encouraged the spread of the doctrine of Mediatrix of all graces by granting the special liturgical feast of "Mediatrix of all graces" to any bishop who desired to celebrate it in his diocese. Benedict XV also continued the unbroken papal consensus in various papal statements where, after stating that Mary redeemed the world together with Christ, he immediately added in one statement: "It is for this reason that all the graces contained in the treasury of the Redemption are given to us through the hands of the same sorrowful Virgin" (*Inter Sodalicia*).

During part of the canonization process of St. Joan of Arc in 1926 (referring to a miracle through the intercession of Joan of Arc that took place at Lourdes), Benedict XV explained that the favors received through the intercession of the saints also come through the mediation of Mary:

> If in every miracle we must recognize the mediation of Mary, through whom, according to God's will, every grace and blessing comes to us, it must be admitted that in the case of one of these miracles [referring to Joan of Arc] the mediation of the Blessed Virgin manifested itself in a very special way. We believe that God so disposed the matter in order to remind the faithful that the remembrance of Mary must never be excluded, even when it may seem that a miracle is to be attributed to the intercession or the mediation of one of the blessed or one of the saints.[10]

• *Pope Pius XI* (1922-1939) several times continued the papal uniformity by making about Mary such statements as: "We have nothing more at heart than to promote more and more the piety of the Christian people toward the Virgin treasurer of all graces at the side of God" (*Cognitum sane*). And also: "Confiding in her intercession with Jesus, the one Mediator of God and man (1 Tim 2:5), who wished to associate his own Mother with himself as the advocate of sinners, as the dispenser and mediatrix of graces..."(*Miserentissimus Redemptor*).

• *Pope Pius XII* (1939-1958), the outstanding Marian pope who defined Mary's Assumption into Heaven, continued in perfect harmony the papal unanimity on Mediatrix of all graces: "And since, as St. Bernard declares, 'it is the will of God that we obtain all favors through Mary,' let everyone hasten to have recourse to Mary..."(*Superiore anno*). And also: "She teaches us all virtues; she gives us her Son and with him all the help we need, for 'God wished us to have everything through Mary'" (*Mediator Dei*).

• *The Second Vatican Council* (under the pontificates of John

XXIII and Paul VI) refered to Mary's authentic title as "Mediatrix" and her role as intercessor of the graces for eternal salvation: "Taken up to heaven she did not lay aside this saving office but by her manifold intercession continues to bring us the gifts of eternal salvation....Therefore the Blessed Virgin is invoked in the Church under the title...Mediatrix" (*Lumen Gentium*, No. 62).

Pope John Paul II on Mary's Mediation

John Paul II has dedicated considerable effort in spreading knowledge and understanding of Mary's role of mediation. In his 1987 Marian encyclical *Mother of the Redeemer*, John Paul II devoted an entire chapter to Mary's "maternal mediation," and explains in this passage how Mary's role as secondary mediator takes on a universal dimension:

> After her Son's departure, her motherhood remains in the Church as maternal mediation: interceding for all her children, the Mother cooperates in the saving work of her Son, the Redeemer of the world. In fact the Council [Vatican II] teaches that the "motherhood of Mary in the order of grace...*will last without interruption* until the eternal fulfilment of all the elect." With the redeeming death of her Son, the maternal mediation of the handmaid of the Lord took on a universal dimension, for the work of redemption embraces the whole of humanity.... Mary's cooperation shares, in its subordinate character, *in the universality of the mediation of the Redeemer*, the one Mediator (*Redemptoris Mater*, No. 40).

Shortly after in the same encyclical, Pope John Paul II granted the Blessed Virgin a new title as "Mediatrix of Mercy" at the second coming of her Son:

> [S]he also has that specifically maternal role of mediatrix of mercy *at his final coming*, when all those who belong to Christ "shall be made alive," when "the last enemy to be destroyed is death" (1 Cor 15:26) (*Redemptoris Mater*, No. 41).

In his commentary on the wedding of Cana (Jn 2), John Paul explained Mary's actions as Mediatrix in uniting humanity with her Son:

> Thus there is a mediation: Mary places herself between her Son and mankind in the reality of their wants, needs, and sufferings. *She puts herself "in the middle,"* that is to say *she acts as a mediatrix not as an outsider, but in her position as mother.* She knows that as such she can point out to her Son the needs of mankind, and in fact, she "has the right" to do so....*The Mother* of Christ presents herself as the *spokeswoman of her Son's will*, pointing out those things which must be done so that the salvific power of the Messiah may be manifested (*Redemptoris Mater*, No. 21).

And in a 1989 papal address, John Paul II referred to Mary as the Mediatrix of graces reflecting the light of Christ to her earthly children: "Enlightened by the fullness of Christ's light, Mary, Mediatrix of graces, reflects him in order to give him to all her children...."[11]

What is the importance of this survey of two centuries of papal statements on the doctrine of Mediatrix of all graces? It is precisely the conformity and the unanimity of the popes of the last two hundred years that bring new certainty and clarity to this pivotal Marian doctrine of Mediatrix of all graces. The popes of the last two centuries, both in the official Church documents and in papal addresses, have assertively taught this Marian truth with a consistency and specificity that, as Pope Leo XIII said referring to its universal acceptance since apostolic times, seems to be explainable by "no other reason...than divine faith."

Theological Conclusions on Mediatrix

Although this Marian doctrine of Mary as Mediatrix of all graces is not yet formally defined, its unquestionable presence in the papal teachings of the ordinary Magisterium bear several significant theological conclusions as formulated by some of the twentieth century's most respected mariologists.[12]

First, the doctrine of Mary as Mediatrix of all graces must receive from the faithful "loyal submission of the will and intellect," which "must be given, in a special way, to the authentic teaching authority of the Roman Pontiff, even when he does not speak *ex cathedra*" (*Lumen Gentium*, No. 25). By its consistent place in the teachings of the ordinary Magisterium, this Marian doctrine of Mediatrix of all graces calls believers to a religious assent of mind and heart to the manifest mind of the Pope.

Secondly, in light of the fact that the doctrine of Mary as Mediatrix of all graces has been universally taught throughout the Church by popes of the last two hundred years and by the bishops in union with them (the ordinary Magisterium), and in virtue of this universal teaching of the Church, the doctrine of Mediatrix of all graces already possesses the *nature* of a defined doctrine of faith (theologically, this can be referred to as *de fide divina ex ordine magisterio*).[13] In other words, Mary as Mediatrix of all graces, represents essential Catholic teaching through the order of the ordinary Magisterium.

This charism of the universal teaching authority of all

bishops who, when in union with the Pope, can exercise the ecclesial element of infallibility, is discussed in Vatican II's *Constitution on the Church* (*Lumen Gentium*, No. 25).

Models of Mary as Mediatrix

There are also several different, though complementary, models and concepts of Mary as Mediatrix of all graces. St. Maximilian Kolbe saw Mary's profoundly intimate relationship with the Holy Spirit, her Divine Spouse, as central to her role as Mediatrix. When the Holy Spirit, the "uncreated Immaculate Conception of God," as Kolbe refers to Him, works to sanctify the world, He does so in profound union with and through Mary, the human, created Immaculate Conception. God's grace, therefore, flows from the Father, through the Son in the Holy Spirit *and* through the intercession of Mary.[14] Hence, as John Paul II confirms in his Marian encyclical, Mary's mediative role is empowered and intimately related to the Holy Spirit, who is the divine Sanctifier.

In terms of a more ecclesial (or church) model, St. Ambrose and Vatican II stressed Mary's image as "Model of the Church." Since all the graces of Redemption are obtained and distributed through the Church, and Mary is the perfect model of the Church, then Mary likewise would appropriately be Co-redemptrix and Mediatrix of graces par excellence in conformity with the Church.[15]

Some of the most prominent mariologists of our century[16] have also proposed the position of Mary being what is called a "secondary physical cause" in the distribution of graces; that, after Jesus, Mary not only wills or in a moral way distributes graces, but also in a physical manner distributes the graces of the Redemption. It was in a physical, incarnational sense that Jesus, the source of all graces, came to us through Mary. So too, it is appropriate that through Mary's physical glorified body the graces of Redemption come to us. Mary's physical instrumentality is also seen at the Visitation, where Mary's physical presence in bringing the presence of the unborn Jesus leads to the sanctification of St. John the Baptist in the womb of Elizabeth (cf. Lk 1:44).

As one author explains: "Once it is granted that the angels and the saints are frequently physical secondary causes of miracles, it seems quite natural to postulate the same power for the Mother of God and in a higher degree."[17] A recent theological explanation of Mary's physical instrumentality in regards to the sacraments is as follows: "Grace begins in the Divine Nature [of Christ], passes through the sacred humanity of Christ (a physical instrument), passes through Mary (also a physical instrument), and finally passes through the sacrament (also a physical instrument)."[18]

There are also several images of Mary as Mediatrix from the realm of authentic Marian private revelation. The Miraculous Medal apparitions (1830), Lourdes (1854), and Fatima (1917), and several other contemporary Marian apparitions, all portray Mary as distributing the graces of God from the opened palms of her immaculate hands. Although not in the realm of public revelation, authentic Marian private revelation seems to confirm the possibility of Mary's physical distribution of graces.

A more domestic model of Mary as Mediatrix of all graces is the image of Mary as "Nursing Mother." As she physically did with her first Child, Mary spiritually takes all humanity to her breast to nourish them with the spiritual milk of supernatural grace.

Regardless of the diversity of these images and concepts regarding Mary's role as Mediatrix of all graces, all authentic images of Mary in this regard will convey the truth that Mary distributes the graces of Jesus in obedience to the Father, in the service of the Son, and in union with the Holy Spirit.

(Note: Some theological objections to Mary as Mediatrix of

all graces will be responded to in Chapter 7: "In Defense of Mary.")

Let us conclude with the words of St. Bernard of Clairvaux who has been rightly called the "Doctor of Mary's Mediation":

> This is the will of Him who wanted us to have everything through Mary.... God has placed in Mary the plenitude of every good, in order to have us understand that if there is any trace of hope in us, any trace of grace, any trace of salvation, it flows from her.... God could have dispensed His graces according to His good pleasure without making use of this channel [Mary], but it was His wish to provide this means whereby grace would reach you.[19]

Notes

1. Cf. St. Augustine, *De S. Virginitate* 6,6.
2. Cf. Carol, *Fundamentals*, p. 29.
3. St. Thomas Aquinas, *ST*, III Q. 26 art. 1.
4. St. Ephraem, Oratio IV, *Ad Deiparam*.
5. Cf. Carol, "Our Lady's Co-Redemption" in *Mariology*, Vol. II, p. 337; Carol, *De Corredemptione B.V. Mariae disquisitio positiva* (Città Vaticana, 1950).
6. Pope Pius XI, Solemn close of 1935 Jubilee Year of Redemption, *L'Observatore Romano*, April 29, 1935.
7. Cf. *Munificentissimus Deus*, (1950); *Mystici Corporis*, 1943; *Ad coeli Reginam*, 1954.
8. John Paul II, *Allocution at the Sanctuary of Our Lady of Alborada in Quayaquil*, given on Jan. 31, 1985, reported in *L'Observatore Romano Supplement* of Feb. 2, 1985 and in English *L'Observatore Romano*, March 11, 1985, p. 7.
9. Carol, Vol. II, Pope Pius VII, *Ampliatio privilegiorum ecclesiae B.V. Virginis ab angelo salutatae, in Fratrum Ordinis Servorum B.V.M. Florentiae*, 1806.
10. *Actes de Benoit XV*, Vol. 2, 1926, E. Druwe.
11. *L'Observatore Romano*, October 2, 1989.
12. Cf. J. Bittremieux, *De mediatione universali B.M. Virginis quoad gratias*, 1926; Armand J. Robichaud, S.M., "Mary, Dispensatrix of all Graces," in Carol, ed., *Mariology*, Vol. 2, 1957; Garrigou-LaGrange, O.P., *Mother of Our Savior and the Interior Life*, Ch. III, p. 235; Roschini, *Mariologia*, Vol. II; Cardinal Lépicier, O.S.M. *Tractatus de B.V.M.*, Romae, 1926; E. Hugon, O.P., *La causalité instrumentale*, Paris, 1929; William Most, *Mary in our Life*, 1956, p. 38.
13. Cf. J. Bittremieux, *De mediatione universali B.M. Virginis quoad gratias*, 1926; Armand J. Robichaud, S.M., "Mary, Dispensatrix of all Graces," in Carol, ed., *Mariology*, Vol. 2, 1957.
14. Cf. Manteau-Bonamy, O.P., ed., *Immaculate Conception and Holy Spirit: The Marian Teachings of Fr. Kolbe*, (Wisconsin: Prow-Franciscan Marytown Press, 1977), Ch. II, III, IV.
15. Cf. St. Ambrose, *Expos. ev. sec. Luc. II*, 7; *Lumen Gentium*, No. 62-65.
16. Cf. Garrigou-LaGrange, O.P. *Mother of Our Savior and the Interior Life*, Ch. III, p. 235; Robichaud, S.M., "Mary, Dispensatrix of all Graces," Carol, ed., *Mariology*, Vol. II; Roschini, *Mariologia*, Vol. II, Cardinal Lépicier, O.S.M. Tractatus de B.V.M., Romae, 1926; E. Hugon, O.P., *La causalité instrumentale*, Paris, 1929; William Most, *Mary in our Life*, 1956, p. 38.
17. Hugin, O.P. *La causalité instrumentale en theologie*, 1907, p. 195.
18. William Most, *Mary in Our Life*, p. 38.
19. St. Bernard, *Hom. in nativit. B.V.M.* n. 7, n.6, n.3-4.

chapter four

The Rosary: The Greatest Marian Prayer

The Rosary is my favorite prayer, a marvelous prayer. Marvelous in its simplicity and depth. It can be said that the Rosary is, in a certain way, a prayer-commentary on the last chapter of the constitution, *Lumen Gentium*, of Vatican II, a chapter which deals with the wonderful presence of the Mother of God in the mystery of Christ and the Church. Against the background of the words, Ave Maria [Hail Mary], there passes before the eyes of the soul the main episodes of the life of Jesus Christ, and they put us in living communication with Jesus through, we could say, His mother's heart. At the same time, our heart can enclose in these decades of the Rosary all the facets that make up the life of the individual, the family, the nation, the Church and all mankind, particularly of those who are dear to us. Thus the simple prayer of the Rosary beats the rhythm of human life.[1]

Thus spoke Pope John Paul II about his favorite prayer, the Rosary. The Holy Father described the tremendous value of the Rosary for the Christian life in an address delivered within the first weeks of his pontificate in 1978. The Rosary does in fact "put us in living communication with Jesus...through His mother's heart" and "beats the rhythm of human life."

The Rosary, the greatest Marian prayer, has been championed by the Church as the most highly recommended prayer form, second only to the liturgical prayer of the Church centering around the holy Sacrifice of the Mass.

As Pope Leo XIII said in one of his eleven encyclicals written exclusively on the Rosary: "Among the various methods and forms of prayer which are devoutly and profitably used in the Catholic Church, that which is called the Rosary is for many reasons to be especially recommended (*Salutaris ille*, December 24, 1883).

The pre-eminence of the Rosary (after liturgical prayer) is also confirmed by Pope Pius XII: "the Rosary, as all know, has pride of place" (*Mediator Dei*, 1947).

What is the Rosary?

The Rosary is a beautiful combination of vocal prayer and meditation that centers upon the greatest Gospel mysteries in the life of Jesus Christ and secondarily in the life of the Mother of Jesus. It is an "incarnational" prayer, a prayer consisting of both vocal and mental prayer that serves to incorporate both body and soul into spiritual communion with Our Lord.

Basic Structure of the Rosary

The basic structure of the complete Rosary consists in the praying of fifteen sets of ten Hail Marys, referred to as decades, with an Our Father prayed at the beginning of each decade. During the praying of each decade of ten Hail Marys, one of the central Gospel mysteries of Jesus Christ is meditated upon. This prayerful pondering of the life of Jesus imitates the spiritual practice of Mary herself who, Scripture tells us, interiorly "made her own" the sacred events in the life of her Son: "Mary kept all these things, pondering them in her heart" (Lk 2:19). What possibly passed unnoticed by others, did not escape the attention of the Mother of Jesus in regards to salvation history. Mary continually pondered the salvific events and mysteries of her Son in her heart.

Technically the term "Rosary" refers to the full fifteen decades, with a Gospel mystery associated with each decade. The fifteen mysteries are categorized into three sets of five mysteries, known as the Joyful, Sorrowful, and Glorious Mysteries. In these three sets of mysteries we prayerfully meditate upon the three great general mysteries of our salvation as accomplished by Our Lord Jesus Christ: the Incarnation, the Redemption and Eternal Life.

The Joyful Mysteries, which center upon the event of the Incarnation of Jesus, consist of: the Annunciation (Lk 1:26f), the Visitation of Mary to Elizabeth (Lk 1:39f), the Birth of Jesus (Lk 2:7, Mt 1:25), the Presentation of Jesus (Lk 2:21f), and the Finding of the Child Jesus in the Temple (Lk 2:42f).

The Sorrowful Mysteries, which focus on the Redemption of Jesus by His Passion and Death, consist of: the Agony in the Garden (Mt 26:36), the Scourging at the Pillar (Jn 19:1), the Crowning with Thorns (Mt 27:29), Jesus' Carrying of the Cross (Jn 19:17), and the Crucifixion of Jesus (Lk 23:33).

The Glorious Mysteries, which center upon the mystery of Eternal Life through the victory of Jesus, consist of: the Resurrection of Jesus (Lk 24:6), the Ascension of Jesus into Heaven (Mk 16:19), the Descent of the Holy Spirit at Pentecost (Acts 2:2f), the Assumption of Mary into Heaven (cf. Ps 131:8; Gen 3:15; Lk 1:28) and the Crowning of Mary as Queen of Heaven (cf. Rev 12:1).

Thus, as one theologian explained about the mysteries of the

Rosary:

> The Rosary is a *Credo* [creed]: not an abstract one, but one concretized in the life of Jesus who came down to us from the Father and Who ascended to bring us back with Himself to the Father. It is the whole of Christian dogma in all its splendor and elevation, brought to us that we may fill our minds with it, that we may relish it and nourish our souls with it.[2]

Commonly in the English language, the term "Rosary" refers to a third of the full Rosary, consisting of five decades or one set of mysteries, whereas expressions such as the "complete Rosary" or "full Rosary" signify the entire fifteen decades. This is not always the case in other cultures and languages. For example, in the French, the term "rosaire" usually designates the complete Rosary and a different word, "chapelet," is used to signify one third of the Rosary.

The Rosary then comprises a beautiful blend of vocal and meditative prayer that leads the person into the joyful, sorrowful, and glorious events of the life of Jesus our Redeemer.

Brief History of the Rosary

Traditionally, the origin of the Rosary is traced back to the person of St. Dominic Guzman (d. 1221), founder of the Dominican Order. St. Dominic had been sent to southern France to preach against the Albigensian heresy which was ravaging the region. The Albigensian heresy denied the infinite goodness and power of God and held that all matter was evil (being a later development of Manichaeism). Albigensianism attacked both Christian morality and Christian doctrine as well, opposing such truths as Creation, the Incarnation, true Redemption and Eternal Life. Since matter was mistakenly conceived as evil, the Albigensians held that God the Son could not truly have taken on a material human nature to redeem humanity.

It was, therefore, as a spiritual instrument to battle the moral and dogmatic errors of Albigensianism (as well as an instrument against future errors and difficulties) that St. Dominic reportedly received, under the inspiration of the Blessed Virgin Mary, a unique combination of preaching and prayer that would constitute the basis of the prayer form later known as the Rosary. One account of how St. Dominic received from the Blessed Virgin the root form of the Rosary was explained by the renowned Dominican theologian Garrigou-LaGrange:

> Our Blessed Lady made known to St. Dominic a kind of preaching till then unknown, which she said would be one of the most powerful weapons against future errors and in future difficulties. Under her inspiration, St. Dominic went into the villages of the heretics, gathered the people, and preached to them the mysteries of salvation—the Incarnation, the Redemption, Eternal Life. As Mary had taught him to do, he distinguished the different kinds of mysteries, and after each short instruction, he had ten Hail Marys recited—somewhat as might happen even today at a Holy Hour. And what the word of the preacher was unable to do, the sweet prayer of the Hail Mary did for hearts. As Mary promised, it proved to be a most fruitful form of preaching.[3]

Although there are several diverse theories as to precisely what St. Dominic contributed to the origins of the Rosary, the basic concept of uniting the praying of Hail Marys with preaching and meditation on the Gospel mysteries of Jesus Christ can most likely be attributed to the founder of the Dominican Order through the specific inspiration of the Blessed Virgin (an inspired beginning to which several papal documents refer).[4]

Rosary Development

After this initial inspiration of the Rosary from the Blessed Virgin to St. Dominic, the structure of the Rosary went through a period of gradual development from the thirteenth to the sixteenth century. One hundred and fifty Hail Marys began to be recited by the laity to model the one hundred and fifty psalms prayed by the monks as contained in the Psalter or Divine Office. The use of beads was incorporated for the counting of the prayers. Gradually, fifteen Our Fathers were added to break up these one hundred and fifty Hail Marys into fifteen sets of ten which we call "decades." This Our Father- and Hail Mary-based prayer form became known as "Our Lady's Psalter." It was an effort to incorporate the laity, the vast majority of which was illiterate, into praying the liturgical prayer of the monks in the monasteries which included the one hundred and fifty Psalms.

The specific Rosary mysteries also went through significant historical development. At given times in the fourteenth and fifteenth centuries, anywhere from fifty to one hundred and fifty mysteries were meditated upon during the reciting of one hundred and fifty Hail Marys (in some cases having one specific mystery for each Hail Mary). Gradually, the number of mysteries was reduced from as many as one hundred and fifty down to fifteen. The first clear historical example of what is basically the Rosary form used today is found in the mid-fifteenth century writings of Alan of Rupe (also known as Alan de la Roche) O.P. (d.1475).[5] Alan of Rupe was a great Dominican propagator of the Rosary devotion and a significant historical force in restoring the practice of the Rosary to the faithful.

Finally, in 1569, in the Apostolic Constitution *Consueverant*

Romani Pontifices, Pope St. Pius V, a Dominican pope, officially approved what is the basic Rosary prayer form of today. By the time of the 1569 official papal approval, the second part of the Hail Mary, an ecclesial prayer added during the Middle Ages, was also present.

Historically, it is noteworthy that only three years later before the Battle of Lepanto in 1572 (when Muslim invaders threatened all of Western civilization), Pope St. Pius V called upon the Christian world to pray the Rosary to aid the smaller Christian naval fleet against the massive Muslim fleet. The somewhat miraculous victory of the Christian fleet was directly attributed by Pius V to the powerful effects of praying the Rosary.

What is essential to the praying structure of the Rosary, as discussed by the many papal documents, are the fifteen Our Fathers and the one hundred and fifty Hail Marys coupled with vocal prayer (at least the word formation by the lips) and meditation on the fifteen Gospel mysteries. Strictly speaking, the only prayers that belong to the essential nature of the Rosary are the fifteen Our Fathers and the one hundred and fifty Hail Marys.

Rosary Diversity

Over time and in diverse cultures, several prayers have been added to the Rosary by the faithful. In several countries (including France, parts of Germany and the United States), the Rosary begins with the Sign of the Cross, the Apostles' Creed, an Our Father, three Hail Marys (oftentimes prayed for an increase in the theological virtues of faith, hope and charity) and a Glory Be to the Father. But this is not always the universal practice. In several Spanish speaking countries, the Rosary ends with these same prayers. In other countries, Italy, for example, these prayers are normally not said at all.

The praying of the Glory Be to the Father at the end of each decade is also not a universal practice, although common in most parts of the world. The addition of the Glory Be was probably an effort to imitate the praying of the psalms of the Divine Office, which end with this same prayer of Trinitarian praise.

At the end of each decade various additional prayers have also been recited by the faithful. Presently, the most universal prayer added to the end of each decade is the one requested by the Virgin Mary during her 1917 apparitions at Fatima, Portugal. During her third apparition of July 13, 1917, Mary appeared under the title of "Our Lady of the Rosary" and asked that the following prayer be said at the end of each decade: "O my Jesus, forgive us our sins, save us from the fires of Hell, lead all souls to Heaven, especially those who are most in need (of Thy mercy)." Many of the faithful from around the world permanently incorporated this prayer request from Our Lady of Fatima at the end of each Rosary decade.

The *Salve Regina* or "Hail Holy Queen," a majestic prayer to Mary as our Queen and Mother of Mercy, was attributed to St. Bernard of Clairvaux (d.1153). The Hail Holy Queen is normally prayed at the end of five decades of the Rosary (or the full fifteen decades). But in a few countries, the Hail Holy Queen is prayed at the beginning of the Rosary, which is the traditional practice of the Dominican Order.

Other various practices in the praying of the Rosary include the one popularized by St. Louis Marie de Montfort in France and by others in German speaking countries, that of adding to the name of Jesus at the end of the first part of the Hail Mary a title or a petition that incorporates the respective mystery. For example, when praying the Sorrowful Mysteries one might add: "...of thy womb, Jesus, agonizing in the garden," for the First Sorrowful Mystery; "...Jesus, crowned with thorns," for the Third Sorrowful Mystery; or "...Jesus, crucified to death," for the Fifth Sorrowful Mystery.

Surely we should appreciate the splendid embellishments of the praying of the Rosary added by the beauty of diversity in the Church, but all additions should serve, and not detract from, the heart of the Rosary, which remains the vocal praying of the Our Fathers and Hail Marys and meditative pondering of the Gospel life of Our Lord and His Mother.[6]

We see historically then that the Rosary is the product of a peaceful combination of both heavenly inspiration and human development as prayed and practiced by the living Church.

(Note: A practical guide on How to Pray the Rosary, with the additional prayers prayed in English speaking countries, appears in the Appendix.)

Basic Qualities of the Rosary

Rosary is Scriptural

In discussing what makes up the essential qualities of the Rosary, we see first of all that the Rosary is by nature a scriptural prayer. Pope Paul VI refers to the Rosary as "the compendium of the entire Gospel" (*Marialis Cultus*, No. 42).

The fifteen mysteries of the Rosary comprise the best possible summary of the Gospel events of the Lord. They start at the beginning of the New Testament salvation history with the Annunciation (Lk 1:26) and recall each pillar Gospel mystery of Our Lord's infancy, passion, and redemptive victory, ending with the glorious effect for the Mother of Jesus (His first and greatest disciple), that of her Coronation in Heaven (Rev 12:1). Hence, the Rosary mysteries provide a sublime but succinct summary of the greatest Gospel mysteries contained in the New Testament.

Beyond the scriptural nature of the Rosary mysteries, the

specific prayers of the Rosary are also essentially scriptural. The Our Father is the celestial prayer revealed by Jesus Christ in answer to the request of the disciples to "teach us how to pray" (Lk 11:2f; Mt 6:7f). The Our Father is the perfect prayer of praise and petition revealed by God the Son made man.

The Hail Mary, for centuries called the "Angelic Salutation," is also fundamentally a scriptural prayer. The first part of the Hail Mary is a joining together of the two scriptural greetings: one to Mary by the Angel Gabriel, "Hail, full of grace, the Lord is with you" (Lk 1:28); and one to Mary by her cousin Elizabeth, "blessed are you among women, and blessed is the fruit of your womb" (Lk 1:42). With the additions of the names of Jesus and Mary, these two scriptural greetings to Mary comprised the entire prayer of the Hail Mary for at least the first twelve centuries.[7]

During the Middle Ages, the Church added the second part of the Hail Mary, the ecclesial prayer to the Mother of God beseeching her intercession for "us sinners," "now" and "at the hour of our death." The second portion of the Hail Mary reflects the humble prayer of sinners for the heavenly aid of the Mother of God in a manner resembling the first recorded Marian prayer, the *Sub Tuum*. Both Marian prayers reflect Mary's divine motherhood and intercessory power which are also scripturally based (cf. Gen 3:15; Lk 1:28; Jn 2:1; Jn 19:26).

By means of both its Gospel mysteries and its scripturally based prayers, the Rosary may rightly be called a "compendium of the entire Gospel."

Rosary is Christ-centered

Another principal quality of the Rosary is that it is a Christ-centered (or Christological) prayer. By means of the Gospel mysteries and of the prayers, the focus of the Rosary is centered first and foremost on the person and life of Jesus Christ and His redemption of the human family. As Pope Paul VI explains in his 1974 Marian document:

> As Gospel prayer, centered on the mystery of the redemptive Incarnation, the Rosary is therefore a prayer with a clearly Christological orientation. Its most characteristic element, in fact, the litany-like succession of Hail Marys, becomes in itself an unceasing praise of Christ, who is the ultimate object both of the angel's announcement and of the greeting of the mother of John the Baptist: "Blessed is the fruit of your womb" (Lk 1:42) (*Marialis Cultus*, No. 46).

We see that thirteen of the fifteen Rosary mysteries are explicitly dedicated to the life of Jesus. As for the last two mysteries, the Assumption and Coronation of Mary, these mysteries illustrate the application of the graces of the victorious Christ to Mary, the first and greatest disciple of the Lord. And in a certain sense, the last two Glorious Mysteries foreshadow what all faithful disciples of the Lord will receive (although to a lesser degree than the Mother of Jesus). The Assumption of Mary foreshadows the Resurrection of the Body which all the faithful await on the last day (cf. Mt 22:29f; Lk 14:14; Jn 6:39). The Coronation of Mary foreshadows the heavenly crown that, as St. Paul tells us, all children of God can expect upon running the race (1 Cor 9:24-25; 2 Tim 4:8). The last two mysteries then are a foretaste of what all Christians can expect in due measure when they remain faithful to the first thirteen mysteries of the Lord.

The prayers of the Rosary are likewise Christ-centered, with Jesus as the source of the Our Father and the ultimate object of praise of the Hail Mary. As Pope Paul VI pointed out, the prayerful repetition of the Hail Marys makes up "an unceasing praise of Christ, who is the ultimate object of both the angel's announcement and the greeting of the mother of John the Baptist."

Rosary: Vocal and Meditative Prayer

A third principal quality of the Rosary is its harmonious blend of vocal prayer and meditation. In one of his eleven encyclicals exclusively on the Rosary, Pope Leo XIII explained that:

> [The Rosary] is comprised of two parts, distinct but inseparable—the meditation on the mysteries and the recitation of the prayers. It is thus a kind of prayer that requires not only some raising of the soul to God but also a particular and explicit attention, so that by reflection upon the things to be contemplated, impulses and resolutions may follow for the reformation and sanctification of life (*Iucunda semper*, 1894).

As was mentioned, the Rosary is an incarnational prayer that encompasses both vocal prayer and mental prayer, both head and heart, both soul and body. The physical use of beads and formation of the words in vocal prayer are important in this body-soul complement of the Rosary. As we count the prayers by the physical use of beads, the soul is freed from the practical distraction of counting and able to focus upon the prayers and meditations.

Beyond just fulfilling this practical need for counting, the physical involvement of the body, coupled with the physical formation of the words (even when sound is not possible), helps to keep the body at the disposition of the soul, to keep the body focused and subordinated to the soul soaring higher in prayer.

St. Louis Marie de Montfort strongly emphasized the value of
physically fingering the beads while in spiritual conversation
with God during Rosary prayer.[8]

Meditation can, therefore, be considered the "soul" of the
Rosary, while vocal prayer (coupled with the physical use of
beads) can be considered the "body" of the Rosary. As one
author succinctly put it, "the beads are there for the sake of the
prayers, and the prayers are there for the sake of the Mysteries."[9]

The combined effect of vocal prayer and meditation makes
up a powerful and efficacious means of spiritual growth, but also
an effective instrument of physical and emotional tranquility.
One author describes both the spiritual and physical/emotional
peace that comes from this vocal-mental prayer harmony of the
Rosary:

> Isn't it fascinating that scientists are now turning to
> meditation in our "hectic" age when so many of us have
> thrown it out? We have discarded one of the most
> powerful of all forms of meditation, the Rosary. It is so
> perfectly designed to fulfill our meditative needs. It is
> physical—our fingers move over the beads. God has
> given His children the gift of the Rosary beads on which
> to count His love. Fifteen mysteries spell it out in a way
> we can understand. The mind, like a velvet bee droning
> over a rose, draws the honey of comfort from the story of
> God. The running rhythm and the repetition, Hail
> Mary, Holy Mary, steady the mind and settle the heart on
> God's work in His powerful mysteries. With Mary's
> glance, through the eyes of the heart, we view it afresh.
> One of the therapies for soldiers who had survived the
> stresses of World War I was, of all occupations, knitting!
> It was recognized that the nervous energy of the body
> passes out through the fingers.... Our worries, tensions,
> joys and pains are surrendered to God with the Rosary as

the rhythmic repetition of the Our Father and the Hail Mary focuses our hearts in peace on the central mysteries of Christ's life, death and glory which alone offer direction and meaning to our lives.[10]

Hence the emotional life as well greatly benefits from the wholistic prayer of the Rosary.

Rosary as a Christian Meditation

What exactly is meditation? Meditation is the prayerful pondering of the mind and heart on some supernatural truth or object. Generally, authentic Christian mediation has at least three basic elements: Consideration, Application and Resolution.[11]

Consideration is when the mind intellectually but prayerfully considers the spiritual subject in question, for example, pondering prayerfully the event of the Annunciation.

Application is when the person in meditative prayer applies the truths of the spiritual subject, for example, a mystery of the Rosary, to one's own spiritual life. It is to answer questions like, "What does the Annunciation have to do with me and my own spiritual life? How do I, like the Virgin of Nazareth in answer to the Angel Gabriel's message, respond to God's daily and oftentimes surprising manifest will?"

Resolution is to make some practical resolve in my own spiritual life based on the truth and application of the Gospel mystery. It is to say, for example, I resolve with the help of God's grace to be more receptive to God's daily will and to meet it with the "fiat" of Mary to the best of my ability.

Although generally there need not be an explicit step by step use of these elements of meditation as just described, the acts of consideration, application and resolution are nonetheless organic parts of authentic Christian meditation and, thereby, parts of the praying of the Rosary.

Some have perceived the Rosary as a monotonous, even boring prayer of repetition that incorporates nothing more than a rather redundant type of vocal prayer. Several popes have responded specifically to this objection to the Rosary. Pope Pius XI responded to the issue of monotony with these words:

> [T]hey are in error who consider this devotion a boresome formula repeated with monotonous and sing-sing intonations....[B]oth piety and love, although always breathing forth the same words, do not, however, repeat the same thing, but they fervently express something ever new which the loving heart always sends forth (*Ingravescentibus malis*).

In a similar voice, Pope Pius XII confirmed:

> [T]he recitation of identical formulas, repeated so many times, rather than rendering the prayer sterile and boring, has on the contrary, the admirable quality of infusing confidence in him who prays, and brings to bear a gentle compulsion on the motherly heart of Mary (*Ingruentium malorum*, 1957).

Even for those who find it challenging to meditate consistently during the praying of the Rosary, the prayerful repetition of vocal prayer is not a fruitless practice, since for vocal prayer to be considered prayer at all, as St. Teresa of Avila points out, it still must be coupled with some attention and devotion.[12] But when meditational prayer is a consistent ingredient in praying the Rosary, this favored Marian prayer becomes a spiritual open door into the revealed Gospel mysteries of God, a means of prayer as unlimited in spiritual depth and efficacy as the mysteries are themselves.

This is why the unlimited nature of Gospel meditation in the Rosary prayer can be a springboard even beyond meditation to authentic Christian contemplation. In this regard, the theologian Garrigou-LaGrange calls the Rosary:

> ...a true school of contemplation. It raises us gradually above vocal prayer and even above reasoned out or discursive meditation. Early theologians have compared the movement of the soul in contemplation to the spiral which certain birds—the swallow, for example—move when they wish to attain to a great height. The joyful mysteries lead to the Passion, and the Passion to the door of Heaven. The Rosary well understood is, therefore, a very elevated form of prayer which makes the whole of dogma accessible to all.[13]

The maxim is therefore true, if correctly understood, that to grow bored of praying the Rosary is to grow bored of meditating on the Gospel.

Fruits of the Rosary

The inestimable spiritual benefits of consistently praying the Rosary are such that they can in no way be comprehensively treated or categorized. At best, we can see indications of the tremendous greatness of this Marian prayer by taking a glimpse of the responses to the Rosary by popes, saints, and even the Mother of Jesus herself in her apparitions to the modern world.

Papal Praise of the Rosary

The popes have been nothing short of superlative in their praises of the Rosary and its spiritual benefit. These vicars of Christ on earth consistently place the Rosary second only to the liturgical prayer of the Church as the most highly recommended prayer form. When one considers the ubiquitous forms of diverse prayer within the universal Church of Christ across the last two thousand years, the popes' placing of the Rosary second only to liturgical prayer bespeaks its sublime spiritual value in the mind of the Church.

Almost every pope from Pope Sixtus IV in 1478 to Pope John Paul II has explicitly praised the Rosary and invited the faithful to make the praying of the Rosary a consistent practice. Further, the popes have tried to encourage the frequent (and specifically the daily) praying of the Rosary by embellishing the praying of the Rosary with generous Church indulgences.

A Church indulgence is a partial or complete pardon for the remaining atonement needed for sin after the guilt and the eternal punishment for sin has been forgiven. If atonement is not made for sin in this life, "temporal punishment" for sin must be expiated in Purgatory (cf. 2 Mac 12:42-46; Mt 12:32; 1 Cor 3:15).

Apart from the negative association that indulgences received in a time of disciplinary abuse during the fifteenth and sixteenth centuries, Church indulgences remain an extremely valuable spiritual gift of the Church, and the popes have been particularly generous in endowing the praying of the Rosary with Church indulgences.

Recent popes have generously granted plenary indulgences (full remission of temporal punishment) for the praying of the Rosary when prayed daily for a month; when prayed as a family twice a month; or whenever the Rosary is prayed in the presence of the Blessed Sacrament. All acts for plenary indulgences must also include Holy Communion, Confession and prayers for the intentions of the Pope and detachment from sin.[14]

The Magisterium has also strongly praised the profound spiritual effects of praying the Family Rosary. Since the Family Rosary is endowed with particularly rich indulgences and most highly recommended, the popes have tried to lead Christian families to the spiritual graces and protection received when the family prays the Rosary together daily. As Pope John Paul II (quoting Pope Paul VI) says in his 1981 document on the Christian family:

> While respecting the freedom of the children of God, the Church always proposed certain practices of piety to the faithful with particular solicitude and insistence.
>
> Among these should be mentioned the recitation of the Rosary: "We now desire, as a continuation of our predecessors, to recommend strongly the recitation of the Family Rosary.... There is no doubt that...the Rosary should be considered as one of the best and most efficacious prayers in common that the Christian family is invited to recite. We like to think, and sincerely hope, that when the family gathering becomes a time of prayer, the Rosary is a frequent and favored manner of praying" (*Familiaris Consortio*, No. 61).

The special means of spiritual protection and spiritual grace received from the daily praying of the Family Rosasry should not be underestimated. This daily practice performed by the Domestic Church is of tremendous spiritual efficacy and is strongly encouraged by the universal Church.

Further, the testimony by the saints over the last half millennium has provided enthusiastic praise of the efficacy of praying the daily Rosary. Saints of the spiritual stature of St.

Teresa of Avila, Doctor of the Church on Prayer, St. Francis de Sales, St. Louis Marie de Montfort, St. Alphonsus Liguori, St. Don Bosco, St. Bernadette, and many more, have not only extolled the ineffable graces received in praying the Rosary daily, but have also identified the Rosary as their favorite prayer.

Rosary in Marian Apparitions

A primary source bespeaking the great spiritual value of the Rosary particularly in our present age is the testimony of the Blessed Virgin herself, in her Marian apparitions to the modern world (a subject treated more fully in Chapter 6).

At Lourdes, France in 1858, Mary invited the world to pray the Rosary first by her own example. In the first Marian apparition to Bernadette Soubirous on February 11, 1858, the visionary reported that Mary herself was giving the example of praying the Rosary: "The Lady dressed in white...ran the beads of hers through her fingers."[15] Bernadette prepared for each of the seventeen following apparitions of Mary by praying the Rosary, a practice also adopted by the surrounding crowds.

At Fatima, Portugal in 1917, Mary appeared to three Portuguese children under the title of Our Lady of the Rosary, so important was this Rosary call to the twentieth century. Our Lady of the Rosary explicitly exhorted the world to the daily praying of the Rosary in order to obtain peace for the world and the end of World War I: "Pray the Rosary every day in order to obtain peace in the world and the end of the war" (May 13, 1981). And in her last Fatima apparition in 1917, Our Lady of the Rosary called the human family to continue always the practice of praying the Rosary daily: "I am the Lady of the Rosary. Always continue to pray the Rosary every day" (October 13, 1917).[16]

More recently, in several reported contemporary apparitions

of Mary, the emphatic Marian call for daily Rosary, and even for the full fifteen decade daily Rosary, for the conversion of the world has reached an historical climax.

In the reported apparitions of Mary at Medjugorje, Bosnia-Hercegovina (presently under Church investigation), the Virgin Mary under the title of Queen of Peace, has requested the daily praying of the full fifteen decade Rosary for both spiritual and global peace. Her reported message of August 8, 1985 bespeaks the spiritual power and protection of the Rosary against Satan:

> Dear children, today I call you to pray against Satan in a special way. Satan wants to work more, now that you know he is active. Dear children, put on your armour against Satan: with Rosaries in your hands, you will conquer.[17]

And on June 25, 1985 (the fourth anniversary of the reported apparitions), the Queen of Peace transmitted the following message:

> I invite you to call on everyone to pray the Rosary. With the Rosary you shall overcome all the adversities which Satan is trying to inflict on the Catholic Church.[18]

Protestant Christians and the Rosary

A final, though diverse, indication of the efficacy and value of the Rosary can be seen today in a new openness, probably as never before in history, by many Protestant Christians to the praying of the Rosary. As summarized by one author:

> Protestants are now coming to recognize the value of the Rosary as instanced by a number of favorable writings,

the formation of Rosary circles in Anglican churches and the active propagation of the Rosary by the Anglican Shrine of Our Lady of Walsingham. A German Lutheran minister, Richard Baumann, stated in the early 1970's: "In saying the Rosary, truth sinks into the subconscious like a slow and heavy downpour. The hammered sentences of the Gospel receive an indelible validity for precisely the little ones, the least, to whom belongs the Kingdom of Heaven…. The Rosary is a long and persevering gaze, a meditation, a quieting of the spirit in praise of God, the value of which we Protestants are learning more and more." A Methodist minister, J. Neville Ward, praises the Rosary as a strong support to prayer and meditation in his book *Five for Sorrow, Ten for Joy* and admits that Protestants have lost much in their neglect of this prayer.[19]

In sum, the Church's Magisterium, the manifest mind of the popes, the writings of the saints, and even the realm of Marian private revelation have singled out the Rosary as not only the greatest Marian prayer, but *the* Marian devotional prayer with primacy of place.

May all disciples of Jesus be able to echo the words common to popes and saints, from St. Teresa of Avila, the Doctor of Prayer, to Pope John Paul II, the present Vicar of Christ, that the Rosary is in principle and practice "my favorite prayer."

Notes

1. Pope John Paul II, Angelus message, October 29, 1978, *L'Observatore Romano*.
2. R. Garrigou-LaGrange, O.P., *Mother of Our Saviour and the Interior Life*, p. 293.
3. R. Garrigou-LaGrange, O.P., p.297.
4. Cf. Very Reverend Msgr. George Shea, "The Dominican Rosary" in *Mariology*, Vol. III, Carol, ed., 1957. For diverse opinions, Michael O'Carroll, C.S.Sp., "Rosary" in *Theotokos*.
5. Cf. A. Walz, O.P., *Compendium Historiae Ordinis Praedicatorum*, ed. 2, Romae, 1948.
6. For more details on the diversity of the Rosary in different cultures, cf. Thurston, "The Rosary" in *The Month*, Vol. 96 1900/II, pp. 636-637; Vol. 1901/I. P. 217; Shea, "The Dominican Rosary" *Mariology*, Vol III, 1961; Attwater, *A Dictionary of Mary*, (New York: Catholic Book Publishing Company, 1985); De Montfort, *Secret of the Rosary*, p. 179.
7. In the 13th century, St. Thomas Aquinas wrote a commentary on the Hail Mary that consisted of a treatment of what we today consider to be only the first part of the prayer concluding with the name, "Jesus."
8. Cf. Louis Marie de Montfort, *Secret of the Rosary*, Ch. 1-3.
9. Maisie Ward, *The Splendor of the Rosary*, 1945, p.11-12.
10. Rev. Gerard McGinnity, *Celebrating with Mary*, (Dublin: Veritas, 1987), p.28.
11. Cf. Blessed Louis of Granada, O.P., *Summa of the Christian Life*, Vol. I.
12. Teresa of Avila, *Interior Castle*, First Mansion.
13. Garrigou-LaGrange, O.P., p.294.
14. *Enchiridion Indulgentiarum*, nn. 395-398.
15. R. Laurentin, *Lourdes, Documents Authentiques* as translated in Alan Heame, *The Happenings at Lourdes,* (London: Catholic Book Club, 1968), pp. 82-131.
16. Kondor, L, ed., *Fatima in Lucia's Own Words: Sr. Lucia's Memoirs*, (Fatima, 1976), pp. 166-168.
17. M. Miravalle, S.T.D., *The Message of Medjugorje: The Marian Message to the Modern World*, (Maryland: University Press of America, 1986), Ch. I.
18. Miravalle, *Message of Medjugorje*, Ch. I.
19. McGinnity, *Celebrating with Mary*, p. 30.

chapter five

The Crowning of Marian Devotion: Consecration to Jesus through Mary

This devotion consists then in giving ourselves entirely to the Blessed Virgin, in order to belong entirely to Jesus through her.[1]

These words by St. Louis Marie de Montfort, the great promulgator of Marian consecration, sum up well both the means and the goal of consecration to Jesus through Mary. Far from being simply an added or isolated Marian piety, consecration to Jesus through Mary represents a crowning of Marian devotion, a new Marian dimension of the Christian life, that has been enthusiastically encouraged by the Church for all the faithful.

What is Marian Consecration?

Marian consecration is fundamentally a promise of love and a gift of self that gives all that the Christian is and does completely to Jesus through Mary's motherly intercession. It is to give oneself entirely to Mary in a self-donation of love that enables the Mediatrix of all graces to use her full intercessory power to keep a person faithful to his or her baptismal promises to Jesus Christ.

Brief History of Marian Consecration

Consecration to Mary has a long and rich tradition in the history of the Church. An early understanding of this gift of self to the Mother of Jesus was seen in the form of being a "servant or slave to the Mother of God." Although more foreign to contemporary usage, the term "servant" or "slave" was not understood in a depersonalizing sense. Rather, it was a succinct expression used by several Church Fathers and Doctors to indicate a whole-hearted dependence on the Mother of Christ and is now generally synonymous with the terms "total consecration" and "total abandonment."

The expression, "slave of Mary" was also modelled in a secondary sense after the scriptural expression used by St. Paul of being a "slave of Jesus Christ" (cf. Rom 1:1; Phil 1:1; 1&2 Tim 1:1; etc.), which likewise is meant as a complete filial (a son- or daughter-like) gift of self.

The Church Doctor St. John Damascene (d.749), referred to himself as a "slave of the Mother of God" and authored the following prayer form of Marian consecration in the eighth century:

O Lady, before you we take our stand. Lady, I call you Virgin Mother of God and to your hope, as to the sure and strongest anchor we bind ourselves; to you we consecrate our mind, our soul, our body, all that we are....[2]

Even before St. John Damascene, the phrase *servus Mariae*

(servant or slave of Mary) can be found in African sermons from the fifth and the sixth centuries. The western saint, St. Idlefonsus of Toledo (d.669), also wrote of being "the servant of the handmaid of the Lord":

> Therefore I am your servant, because your Son is my Lord. Therefore you are my Lady because you are the handmaid of my Lord. Therefore I am the servant of the handmaid of my Lord, because you, my Lady, have become the Mother of my Lord....[3]

The common practice of referring to oneself as a "slave of Mary" or "servant of Mary" was customary as early as the seventh century. It was used in Ireland at least by the ninth century and was given official Church approbation as manifested by the approval of the community of the "Servites of Mary," a religious order in the thirteenth century.

Several popes have likewise proclaimed themselves "slave of the Mother of God," including Pope John VII (d.707), Pope Nicholas IV (d.1292) and Pope Paul V (d.1621).

The great scholastic theologian-saints, St. Anselm of Canterbury (d.1109) and St. Bernard of Clairvaux (d.1153) applied to themselves the same title of slave of the Mother of God, and the latter added these words regarding the practice of giving all to Mary:

> Whatever you are about to offer, remember to commend it to Mary, so that through the same channel whence grace flowed, it may return to the giver of grace.[4]

By the sixteenth and seventeenth centuries, consecration to Mary under its various forms had spread throughout all of Catholic Europe.[5] Note that in all these early forms of Marian consecration, it was union with Christ by imitating and giving oneself to *His Handmaid* that was the final goal of their service to the Mother of the Lord.

St. Louis Marie de Montfort

But even with this solid Church tradition of giving oneself to Jesus through Mary, Marian consecration reached new heights and promulgation through the tireless work of its greatest advocate, St. Louis Marie Grignon de Montfort (1673-1716). St. Louis Marie de Montfort was an indefatigable preacher of "Total Consecration to Jesus through Mary" throughout the regions of France and beyond. For his ceaseless preaching and retreats on Marian consecration, De Montfort, who walked the 1,000 mile trip to Rome to submit his work for papal approval, was named by Pope Clement XI as "Apostolic Missionary." De Montfort later wrote down the substance of his inspired preachings and sermons in the book, *True Devotion to Mary,* a manuscript which for more than one hundred years after his death was locked up in a trunk, only to be discovered in 1842 by a De Montfort priest.

The heart of De Montfort's classic work on *True Devotion to Mary* consists of an act of formal consecration or promise of self to the Mother of Jesus, so that through Mary's intercession the Christian may be completely and totally consecrated to Jesus Christ and faithful to his baptismal promises. As De Montfort explains:

> All our perfection consists in being conformed, united and consecrated to Jesus Christ; and therefore the most perfect of all devotions is, without any doubt, that which the most perfectly conforms, unites, and consecrates us to Jesus Christ. Now, Mary being the most conformed of all creatures to Jesus Christ, it follows that, of all

devotions, that which most consecrates and conforms the soul to Our Lord is devotion to His Holy Mother, and that the more a soul is consecrated to Mary, the more it is consecrated to Jesus.

Hence it comes to pass that the most perfect consecration to Jesus Christ is nothing else than a perfect and entire consecration of ourselves to the Blessed Virgin and this is the devotion I teach; or, in other words, a perfect renewal of the vows and promises of holy Baptism.[6]

Total consecration to Mary thereby allows the one who is most conformed to Jesus Christ, and who is also Spiritual Mother and Mediatrix of all graces, to intercede for the Christian to be united intimately with her Son and to be true to the baptismal promises of the Christian faith.

Marian consecration is not simply an added devotion or prayer, but rather, a crowning of devotion to Mary that invites the Mother of Jesus and her powerful intercession into every aspect of the Christian's life, with her constant efforts to unite us to her Son Our Lord, Jesus Christ. As an introduction to *True Devotion* explains:

St. Louis de Montfort was the one to whom it was given to explain thoroughly the path "to Jesus through Mary" and to shape it into a definite method of spiritual life. He does not propose some special or "extra prayers," but rather, a devotion which essentially consists of one single act which, under various formulas and conditions, we apply to our whole life, both interior and exterior. This devotion leads to a permanent disposition of living and acting habitually in dependence on Mary; it embraces one's entire life, not just one's prayer times or specifically religious acts.[7]

The eminent theologian Fr. Garrigou-LaGrange, O.P. described the various stages of Marian devotion and designated consecration to Mary as the "highest degree" of authentic Marian devotion:

> Like the other Christian virtues, true devotion [to Mary] grows in us with charity, advancing from the stage of the beginner to that of the more proficient, and continuing up to the stage of the perfect. The first degree or stage is to pray devoutly to Mary from time to time, for example, by saying the Angelus when the bells ring. The second degree is one of more perfect sentiments of veneration, confidence and love; it may be manifest by the daily recitation of the Rosary—five decades or all fifteen. In the third degree, the soul gives itself fully to Our Lady by an act of consecration so as to belong altogether to Jesus through her...this act of consecration consists in promising Mary to have constant filial recourse to her and to live in habitual dependence on her, so as to attain to a more intimate union with our Blessed Lord and through Him with the Blessed Trinity present in our souls.[8]

Marian consecration, therefore, should not to be conceived as solely a new devotion or an extra set of prayers. It is, rather, a new Marian way of life that invites the Mother of Jesus into all aspects of Christian life, allowing her to use her full power of intercession to keep us in communion with the Lord.

Let us examine the specific prayer of Marian consecration written by De Montfort and still in very popular usage throughout the world today:

> I, (name), a faithless sinner, renew and ratify today in your hands, O Immaculate Mother, the vows of my Baptism; I renounce forever Satan, his pomps and works;

and I give myself entirely to Jesus Christ, the Incarnate
Wisdom, to carry my cross after Him all the days of my
life, and to be more faithful to Him than I have ever been
before.

In the presence of all the heavenly court, I choose you this
day for my Mother and Mistress [Queen]. I deliver and
consecrate to you, as your slave, my body and soul, my
goods, both interior and exterior, and even the value of
all my good actions, past, present, and future; leaving to
you the entire and full right of disposing of me, and all
that belongs to me, without exception, according to your
good pleasure, for the greater glory of God, in time and
eternity. Amen.[9]

De Montfort's consecration prayer has a strong Christological
focus, with a renewal of the most important Christian vows to
Jesus Christ, the vows of sacramental Baptism. The Christian
renounces Satan and gives himself entirely to Jesus Christ, in
order to carry his cross and ever to increase in fidelity to Christ.

The prayer goes on to consecrate the person to Mary as
Spiritual Mother and Queen (Mistress), giving to Mary all that
the person is and does for God's greater glory. It is a self-
donation, as St. Louis Marie explains, of "all that we are in the
order of nature and in the order of grace and all that may become
ours in the future in the orders of nature, grace, and glory."

Another spiritual effect of this Marian consecration allows
for Mary as Mediatrix of all graces and Mother of the Mystical
Body to distribute a person's offerings and merits so as to benefit
best the Body of Christ. The distribution of spiritual benefits is
not from our limited earthly perspective, but from the perspective of the Mother of Jesus who is Mother of the Mystical Body.
As one author explains:

In this practice of complete dependence on Mary, there may be included—and St. Louis Marie de Montfort invites us to it—the resignation into Mary's hands of everything in our good works that is communicable to other souls, so that she may make use of it in accordance with the will of her Divine Son and for His glory.[10]

It should also be noted that although consecration to Mary represents the crowning of Marian devotion, it should in no sense be considered either as a sign of or reward for spiritual perfection. Rather, it is a *means* of Christian perfection that calls for a prudent spiritual preparation, without ever presupposing sanctity. For example, Marian consecration is certainly inferior to the reception of Holy Eucharist, and yet even young children properly and rightfully partake of the Bread of Life at the Sacrifice of the Mass.

Theological Foundations

The solid theological foundations for an act of consecration to Jesus through Mary lie in the Marian doctrines of Spiritual Motherhood and Mediatrix of all graces. De Montfort states:

[T]he Most High has made her [Mary] sole treasurer of His treasures and the sole dispenser of His graces to enable, to exalt, and to enrich who she wishes.... It was through her that Jesus Christ came to us, and it is through her that we must go to Him. If we fear to go directly to Jesus Christ, our God, whether because of His Infinite greatness or because of our vileness or because of our sins, let us boldly implore the aid and intercession of Mary, our Mother. She is good, she is tender, she has nothing in her austere and forbidding, nothing too sublime and too brilliant. In seeing her, we see our pure nature. She is not the sun, which by the brightness of its rays blinds us because of our weakness; but she is fair and gentle as the moon (Cant 6:9), which receives the light of the sun, and tempers it to make it more suitable to our capacity. She is so charitable that she repels none of those who ask her intercession, no matter how great of sinners they have been; for, as the saints say, never has it been heard since the world was the world that anyone has confidently and perseveringly had recourse to our Blessed Lady and yet has been repelled.[11]

As Spiritual Mother and Mediatrix of all graces, Mary has the God-given task of uniting her earthly children with her first Child. The specific act of Marian consecration both recognizes and utilizes these Marian roles in the order of grace:

Consecration to Our Lady is a practical form of recognition of her universal mediation and a guarantee of her special protection. It helps us to have continual child-like recourse to her and to contemplate and imitate her virtues and her perfect union with Christ.[12]

Moreover, a true act of Marian consecration grants Mary the freedom to use her full power of intercession in the sanctification and spiritual protection of her earthly children. The Blessed Virgin, in imitation of the heavenly Father, must respect our free will. Mary, as Spiritual Mother, can intercede on behalf of the Christian only to the extent that each one freely allows her to do so. When a person then consecrates himself or herself to Mary, this free and total gift of self to Mary allows the Mother of Jesus to use her *complete* God-given power of intercession to sanctify the person in the graces of Jesus Christ and to provide him or her with spiritual protection from the pomps and works of Satan.

Marian consecration completely opens the door to the powerful means of union with Christ given to Mary, Mother of the Church.

Let us again recall the words of the Second Vatican Council that Mary's God-given task of mediation never diminishes or overshadows the task of Jesus Christ the one Mediator, but rather shows His power and fosters intimate union with Him:

> Mary's function as mother of men in no way obscures or diminishes this unique mediation of Christ, but rather shows its power. But the Blessed Virgin's salutary influence on men originates not in any inner necessity but in the disposition of God. It flows forth from the superabundance of the merits of Christ, rests on his mediation, depends entirely upon it and draws all its power from it. It does not hinder in any way the immediate union of the faithful with Christ but on the contrary fosters it (*Lumen Gentium*, No. 60).

Kolbe's "Consecration to the Immaculata"

A more contemporary Marian apostle spreading the call for Marian consecration is the Franciscan priest and Auschwitz hero, St. Maximilian Kolbe. St. Maximilian Kolbe presents a rich mariology that centers around Mary as the "Immaculata" (based on her self-revelation at Lourdes, "I am the Immaculate Conception") and the Holy Spirit, to whom Kolbe refers as the "Uncreated Immaculate Conception" (proceeding from the perfect divine love between the Father and the Son).

St. Maximilian points out the profound, sublime union between Mary, the human Immaculate Conception and the Holy Spirit, the divine, uncreated Immaculate Conception, in the bringing of grace to the human family. Kolbe writes:

> The union between the Immaculata and the Holy Spirit is so inexpressible, yet so perfect, that the Holy Spirit acts only by the Most Blessed Virgin His Spouse. This is why she is the Mediatrix of all grace given by the Holy Spirit. And since every grace is a gift of God the Father through the Son and by the Holy Spirit, it follows that there is no grace which Mary cannot dispose of as her own, which is not given to her for this purpose.[13]

Because of Mary's intimate union with the Holy Spirit in the sanctification of humanity, Kolbe sees consecration to Mary as the means by which the human family can be turned back to God, to be "conquered for the Kingdom of God" through the Immaculata: "The Immaculata must conquer the whole world for herself, and each individual soul as well, so that she can bring all back to God."[14]

Kolbe, much like De Montfort, desired every person to renew their baptismal promises by making a total consecration to the Immaculata. As Kolbe preached on Easter Sunday of 1937:

> We were born again in Baptism, which washed away our sins...How can we dispose ourselves so as to receive the greatest possible influx of grace? Let us consecrate ourselves to the Immaculata. Let her prepare us herself. Let her receive her Son in us. This is the most perfect means, the one Jesus prefers, and the one that will afford us the most abundant fruits of grace.[15]

We see with St. Louis Marie de Montfort and the more recent St. Maximilian Kolbe that the ultimate goal of Marian consecration is greater fidelity, union, and love of Jesus Christ in a renewal of the foundational baptismal vows of Christian faith—a gift of self to Jesus through Mary.

Marian Consecration in Modern Papal Teaching

The popes of the nineteenth and twentieth centuries have enthusiastically endorsed and encouraged consecration to Mary, both by word and by example. Specific papal encouragement has been directed to De Montfort's book and to his corresponding Marian spirituality contained in *True Devotion to Mary*. A nearly unprecedented support for an individual spiritual writing has been offered by the popes of the last one hundred fifty years in encouraging the faithful to read *True Devotion to Mary* and to make the total consecration to Jesus through Mary.

• *Pope Pius IX* declared *True Devotion to Mary* to be free from all doctrinal error and referred to De Montfort's devotion to Mary as the "best and most acceptable form of devotion" to the Blessed Virgin.

• *Pope Leo XIII* encouraged all faithful to make De Montfort's act of consecration by granting a Church indulgence for those who would do so. Pope Leo XIII also beatified De Montfort in 1888.

• *Pope St. Pius X* manifested an exceptional appreciation of the writings of the French Marian apostle and made several efforts to encourage the faithful to read and to practice the Marian spirituality of *True Devotion*. St. Pius X declared his dependence on De Montfort's writing by his own Marian encyclical, *Ad diem illum* and granted a plenary indulgence *in perpetuum* (perpetual) for those who recite De Montfort's formula of Marian consecration. He further granted an apostolic blessing to anyone who merely read *True Devotion*, so much did this Holy Father desire the Catholic world to receive and practice total consecration to Mary.[16]

• *Pope Benedict XV* declared the practice of making the consecration to Mary and its corresponding devotion to be "of great unction and high authority."[17]

• *Pope Pius XI* spoke personally of De Montfort's *True Devotion*: "I have practiced this devotion ever since my youth."

• *Pope Pius XII* canonized De Montfort in 1947 and declared his Marian spirituality to be "consuming, solid and right." He referred to De Montfort as the guide "who leads you to Mary and from Mary to Jesus...he is incontestably one of those who has worked the most ardently and the most efficaciously to make Mary loved and served."[18]

• *Pope John Paul II*, more than any pope, has manifested an appreciation of consecration to Mary and of the spirituality of True Devotion by his spoken and written words. So central is the spirit of Marian consecration to this Vicar of Christ that his very papal motto, "Totus Tuus (I am entirely yours)," is taken from De Montfort's short form prayer of Marian consecration.

In his 1987 Marian encyclical *Redemptoris Mater*, Pope John Paul II discusses the characteristics of "authentic Marian spirituality and devotion" and singles out amidst the rich history in the Church of Marian spirituality the writings of St. Louis Marie de Montfort:

> I would like to recall, among the many witnesses and teachers of this spirituality, the figure of Saint Louis Marie Grignon de Montfort, who proposes consecration to Christ through the hands of Mary, as an effective means for Christians to live faithfully their baptismal commitments. I am pleased to note that in our own time too new manifestations of this spirituality and devotion are not lacking (*Redemptoris Mater*, No. 48).

On a more personal note, John Paul II said the following

words about *True Devotion* in an address to the De Montfort Fathers:

> The reading of this book [*True Devotion*] was a decisive turning point in my life. I say "turning point," but in fact it was a long inner journey.... This "perfect devotion" is indispensable to anyone who means to give himself without reserve to Christ and to the work of Redemption.[19]

Papal Consecration of the World to the Immaculate Heart of Mary

Beyond the specific De Montfort call to Marian consecration, recent popes, as the spiritual fathers of all peoples, have consecrated the entire human family to the maternal care and protection of Mary. The action by some popes has been undertaken at least in partial response to the 1917 Marian apparitions at Fatima.

During the third Fatima apparition of July 13, 1917, the Blessed Virgin asked the Holy Father to consecrate Russia to her Immaculate Heart as a remedy for the errors of Russia that would cause various wars and persecutions of the Church:

> ...I shall come to ask for the consecration of Russia to my Immaculate Heart, and the Communion of Reparation on First Saturdays. If my requests are heeded, Russia will be converted and there will be peace; if not, she will spread her errors throughout the world, causing wars and persecutions of the Church. The good will be martyred, the Holy Father will have much to suffer, various nations will be annihilated. In the end, my

Immaculate Heart will triumph. The Holy Father will consecrate Russia to me, and she will be converted, and a period of peace will be granted to the world.[20]

The term "Immaculate Heart of Mary" refers to the maternal heart of Mary from which, in part, the incarnate physical heart of Jesus came. But beyond just the material aspect, the heart of Mary formally symbolizes the very person of Mary and all the grace, sanctity and love that flows from the Mother of Jesus to the human family. Scripturally, the word "heart" bespeaks the whole person. And as Mary is always that pure channel of grace that flows from and to Jesus, her Immaculate Heart is the perfect channel to the Christ's Sacred Heart, source and symbol of the infinite love of God for humanity.

Thereby, several popes have sought in varying degrees to comply with the request of Our Lady of Fatima to consecrate Russia to Mary's Immaculate Heart and, beyond Russia, to consecrate the entire world to Mary.

On October 31, 1942 Pope Pius XII in a radio broadcast to pilgrims at Fatima (on the silver jubilee of the apparitions), consecrated the world to the Immaculate Heart of Mary:

To you and to your Immaculate Heart in this tragic hour of human history, we commit, we entrust, we consecrate not only holy Church, the mystical body of your Jesus, which suffers and bleeds in so many places, and is afflicted in so many ways, but also the entire world torn by violent discord, scorched in a fire of hate, victim of its own iniquities....[21]

On December 8th of the same year, Pope Pius XII repeated the consecration and made an allusion to Russia in the text. In his 1952 encyclical *Sacro vergente anno*, Pius XII dedicated and consecrated "all the peoples of Russia to the same Immaculate

Heart."[22]

Later, after proclaiming Mary as "Mother of the Church" at the Second Vatican Council, Pope Paul VI renewed Pius XII's consecration of the world to the Immaculate Heart of Mary: "We also entrust the whole human race for its protection, its difficulties and anxieties, its legitimate aspirations and ardent hopes to the guardianship of the heavenly Mother."[23]

And on the fiftieth anniversary of Fatima, May 13, 1967, Pope Paul VI visited Fatima and issued the Marian exhortation, *Signum Magnum* (*A Great Sign*), in which he exhorted *all the faithful* to renew personally their consecrations to the Immaculate Heart of Mary:

> [W]e exhort all the sons of the Church to renew personally their consecration to the Immaculate Heart of the Mother of the Church and to bring alive this most noble act of veneration through a life ever more consonant with the divine will and in a spirit of filial service to, and of devout imitation of, their heavenly Queen.[24]

On March 25, 1984, Pope John Paul II (who was shot on the 67th anniversary of Fatima on May 13, 1987 as was prophesied in the order of future suffering of the Holy Father) invited all bishops of the world to join him in formally consecrating the entire world, including Russia, to the Immaculate Heart of Mary in fulfillment of the Fatima request of 1917. The beautiful, long prayer of consecration entrusted the world to the Immaculate Heart of Mary and petitioned Mary to intercede in delivering the world from the multi-form evils that presently threaten its spiritual and physical well-being.[25] John Paul's consecration of the world to the Immaculate Heart of Mary in 1984 in union with many bishops throughout the world satisfied the Fatima request of 1917. Many contemporaries associate the remarkable and relatively bloodless fall of Eastern European communism in recent times to the papal consecration of the world to the Immaculate Heart of Mary by Pope John Paul II.

John Paul II's "Filial Entrustment to the Mother of Christ"

Further, Pope John Paul II offers a rich theology for personal Marian consecration in his 1987 encyclical *Redemptoris Mater* (*Mother of the Redeemer*). Here the Pope discusses what he calls a "filial entrustment to the Mother of Christ." For his theology of Marian consecration or entrustment, John Paul returns to the foot of the Cross (Jn 19:26).

It is at Calvary that Jesus gave Mary as Spiritual Mother to John and beyond John, to every "beloved disciple." As the Pope states: "Mary's motherhood, which becomes man's inheritance, is a gift: *a gift which Christ himself makes* personally to every individual" (*Redemptoris Mater*, No. 45).

How then does John, the beloved disciple, respond to this gift of Mary's motherhood? The Gospel records John's response: "And from that hour the disciple took her into his own home" (Jn 19:27). John, then, becomes an example of how every beloved disciple of the Lord should respond to Jesus' gift of Mary's spiritual motherhood, a gift delivered from the Cross: to take Mary into our own homes.

The specific way Christians should take Mary "into their homes" is by entrusting themselves, by offering themselves as spiritual sons and daughters to their Christ-given Mother:

The Marian dimension of the life of a disciple of Christ is expressed in a special way precisely through this filial entrusting to the Mother of Christ.... Entrusting himself to Mary in a filial manner, the Christian, like the Apostle John, "welcomes" the Mother of Christ "into his own home..." (*Redemptoris Mater*, No. 45).

Pope John Paul II goes on to explain that the word "home" refers to the spiritual life, the inner life of the believer. This son- or daughter-like act of Marian entrusting invites the Mother of Jesus into the spiritual life of the Christian, allowing Mary to exercise her unifying power of grace between the faithful and her divine Son. As the Pope describes, the Christian who entrusts himself to Mary:

> ...brings her [Mary] into everything that makes up his inner life, that is to say into his human and Christian "I": he *"took her to his own home."* Thus the Christian seeks to be taken into that "maternal charity" with which the Redeemer's Mother "cares for the brethren of her Son," "in whose birth and development she cooperates" in the measure of the gift proper to each through the power of Christ's Spirit (*Redemptoris Mater*, No. 45.)

We see then in the manifest minds of recent popes an enthusiastic and consistent encouragement to the faithful to consecrate or "filially entrust" themselves to the Mother of Christ, and to benefit from the rich spiritual fruits of this new Marian dimension of Christian discipleship.

Marian Consecration and Scapular Devotion

Before concluding our discussion on Marian consecration, brief reference should be made to a form of Marian devotion with significant theological and spiritual complementarity to consecration to Mary. This is the practice of the Brown Scapular devotion. The Brown Scapular (*scapula*, Latin for shoulder) consists of two small pieces of cloth connected by strings and worn over the shoulders as a symbol of protection of and devotion to the Blessed Virgin.

The Brown Scapular devotion originated in an apparition of the Blessed Virgin Mary to St. Simon Stock (1247-1265), a thirteenth century Prior General of the Carmelite Order. A Carmelite tradition records the event as follows:

> The Blessed Virgin appeared to him [St. Simon Stock] with a multitude of angels, holding in her blessed hands the Scapular of the Order. She said: "This will be for you and for all Carmelites the privilege, that he who dies in this will not suffer eternal fire" that is, he who dies in this will be saved.[26]

The wearing of the Brown Scapular (brown to designate association with the brown habit of the Carmelites) offers the "scapular promise" that those who faithfully wear it will not suffer the eternity of Hell and, through the intercession of Mary, will attain the graces of final perseverance.

The theological foundations for the Scapular devotion are similar to that of Marian consecration, namely, the Spiritual Motherhood of Mary in her ability to intercede for her children for, what Vatican II refers to as, the "gifts of eternal salvation" (*Lumen Gentium*, No. 62).

Further, as Mediatrix of all graces, Mary can grant the graces necessary for salvation to those who *faithfully* wear the Scapular as an external symbol of their internal devotion and dependence on the Mother of Jesus. In recognizing the authentic value of Scapular devotion, we must dismiss immediately any formalism, that is, simply the physical wearing of the Scapular without any interior intention to love and serve God. The external wearing of the Scapular must be a reflection of a person's internal efforts of mind and heart to serve God, to love Mary, and to be true to the responsibilities of the Church and to one's state in life. As one

Carmelite author points out:

> As a sign of consecration to Mary, the Scapular is a reminder of the spiritual prerogatives enjoyed by her in the economy of the redemption, and it is a pledge that her role be activated in favor of the wearer of the Scapular. In relation to its wearer, the Scapular is a sign that one has resolved to dedicate himself to the service of Christ and Mary according to his station in life...the Scapular does not provide an escape from the ordinary duties of Christianity, but is rather an incentive to undertake them with fervor and exactitude in the knowledge that one thus prepares himself to arrive at the final goal of the Christian life, union with God in eternity.[27]

But this is not to underestimate the power of Scapular devotion in its ability to allow Mary to intercede for the graces of final perseverance in situations that may appear hopeless from a human perspective. Pope Pius XII spoke of the powerful spiritual effects of wearing the Scapular in the following discourse:

> How many souls even in circumstances which, humanly speaking, were beyond hope, have owed their final conversion and their eternal salvation to the Scapular which they were wearing! How many more, thanks to it, have experienced the motherly protection of Mary in dangers of body and soul.[28]

A balance in an authentic Scapular devotion is achieved, therefore, by avoiding any formalism, and at the same time, by not underestimating the spiritual power present in this symbol of true Marian love and devotion.

Included in the Scapular devotion is the belief that Mary's

intercessory power may be expected in Purgatory by all those who have worn the Scapular in faith (along with the further conditions of having practiced chastity according to one's state in life and prayers designated by one's confessor for this intention). This spiritual benefit of wearing the Scapular, called the "Sabbatine privilege," is traditionally traced back to a Marian apparition to Pope John XXII in 1322. Pope John XXII then reportedly promulgated a bull stating that the faithful wearer of the Scapular who also fulfills the above mentioned conditions would be released from Purgatory on the first Saturday after death. Because of the allusion to Saturday, this Marian Scapular privilege has been called the "Sabbatine privilege."

Apart from questions surrounding the origins of the Sabbatine privilege, numerous subsequent papal documents have confirmed the legitimacy of the privilege of Mary, on her designated day of Saturday, to intercede in an accentuated way for the holy souls in Purgatory who faithfully wear the Scapular during their earthly life.[29]

The Scapular, then, is an external symbol of Marian devotion and dependency, of a continual Marian prayer that acknowledges Mary's intercessory role throughout this life and also in the purification of Purgatory that prepares the Christian for eternal life with God. When its symbolism is correctly understood, the Scapular can become a physical sign of the complete gift of self that takes place in authentic Marian consecration. We can see, therefore, the great complementarity between Marian consecration and the proper understanding of the Brown Scapular devotion.

The spiritual benefit of Scapular devotion, while avoiding any formalistic misconception of its fruits, is well summarized by Pope Pius XII in a 1950 Apostolic letter:

> We are not concerned here with a light or passing matter, but with the obtaining of eternal life itself which is the

substance of the promise of the most Blessed Virgin which has been handed down to us.... But not for this reason may they who wear the Scapular think they can gain eternal salvation while remaining slothful and negligent of spirit, for the Apostle warns us: "In fear and trembling shall you work out your salvation" (Phil 2:12).[30]

Spirit of Marian Consecration

We can synthesize the interior nature and spirit of Marian consecration in the De Montfort formula: "to do all our actions through Mary, with Mary, in Mary, and for Mary: so that we may do them all the more perfectly through Jesus, with Jesus, in Jesus, and for Jesus."[31]

Marian consecration should never be seen as a gift of love and self that stops solely with Mary, but a consecration of self that will always end in the heart of Christ Himself. As De Montfort describes, doing all for Mary does not mean "that we take her for the last end of our services, for that is Jesus Christ alone; but we take her for our proximate end, our mysterious means, and our easy way to go to Him...."[32]

Let us conclude with a modern prayer of Marian consecration written by Pope John Paul II during the 1983 Holy Year of Redemption to be used by Christian families in giving themselves completely to Jesus through Mary:

Most Holy Virgin, Mother of God and of the Church, to your Immaculate Heart we today consecrate our family. With your help, we entrust and consecrate ourselves to the Divine Heart of Jesus in order to be with you and with Him in the Holy Spirit, completely and always entrusted and consecrated to the will of the heavenly Father. Amen.[33]

Notes

1. St. Louis Marie de Montfort, *True Devotion to Mary*, Ch.I, No. 121.
2. St. John Damascene, *Hom. I in dorm.*, in PG, 96, 720A.
3. St. Idlefonsus of Toledo, *De virginitate sanctae Mariae*, ed., V.G. Blance, Madrid 1937. Cf. O'Carroll, "Consecration," *Theotokos*, p.109.
4. Cf. St. Bernard of Clairvaux, *In Assumptione B.V.M.*, Sermo IV, in PL 183, 428.
5. For a brief history of consecration, cf. O'Carroll, "Consecration" in *Theotokos*.
6. De Montfort, *True Devotion*, II, Ch I. No. 120
7. De Montfort, Introduction, *True Devotion*, tr. by Father Fredrich Faber, Tan Books, 1985.
8. Garrigou-LaGrange, O.P., *Mother of Our Savior and the Interior Life*, tr. Bernard Kelly, C.S.Sp., Golden Eagle Book, Dublin, Ireland, 1948.
9. De Montfort, *True Devotion*, supplement, Act of Consecration.
10. Garrigou-LaGrange, O.P., *Mother of the Savior*, p.300.
11. De Montfort, *True Devotion*, I, I, 44; I, II, 85.
12. Garrigou-LaGrange, O.P., *Mother of Our Saviour*, p.300.
13. H.M. Manteau-Bonamy, O.P., *Immaculate Conception and the Holy Spirit, Marian Teachings of Father Kolbe*, Letter to Fr. Mikolujczyk, July 28, 1935.
14. Manteau-Bonamy, *Immaculate Conception*, p.107.
15. Manteau-Bonamy, *Immaculate Conception*, p.108.
16. For a summary of papal pronouncements on *True Devotion*, cf. "Marian Consecration" in *Mariology*, Vol. III.
17. *Acta Apostolicae Sedis*, (*Acts of the Apostolic See*) Vol. 8 (1916) p.172.
18. *Acta Apostolicae Sedis*, Vol. 39 (1947) p.410-411.
19. De Montfort, Introductory pages, *True Devotion*, Tan Publishers, 1985.
20. Louis Kondor, S.V.D., ed., *Fatima in Lucia's Own Words: Sister Lucia's Memoirs*, Fourth Memoir, p.162.
21. *A.A.S.* 34 (1942) p.251-252.
22. *A.A.S.* 44 (1952) p.343.
23. *A.A.S.* 56 (1964) p.1017.
24. *A.A.S.* 59 (1967) p.475; for summary of papal consecration, df. "Consecration" in O'Carroll, ed., *Theotokos*.
25. Author was present at consecration ceremony and translated the consecration prayer from the original Italian.
26. F.M. Xiberta, O. Carm., *De Visione Sancti Simonis Stock* (Rome, 1950) cf. Christian Cerake, O. Carm. "The Scapular Devotion," *Mariology*, Vol. 3, p. 128.
27. Christian Ceroke, O. Carm, "The Scapular Devotion," *Mariology*, Vol. III, p. 137.
28. Pope Pius XII, *Discourses and Radio Broadcasts*, Vol. 12 (1950-51) p. 165.
29. Cf. Ceroke, Scapular Devotion, *Mariology*, Vol. III.
30. Pius XII, *Neminem profecto latet*, *A.A.S.* Vol. 42, 1950, p. 390-391
31. De Montfort, *True Devotion*, No. 257.

32. De Montfort, *True Devotion*, No. 265.
33. John Paul II issued this prayer on December 8, 1983 during the 1983-84 Holy Year of Redemption; it has been translated from the Italian by Lysbeth Miravalle.

chapter six

Mary in Private Revelation

We exhort you to listen with simplicity of heart and honesty of mind to the salutary warnings of the Mother of God....

> Pope John XXIII, February 18, 1959
> Closing of the Marian Year

Contemporary humanity finds itself at the climax of what has been called the "Age of Mary." The last two centuries have received more Church-approved Marian apparitions than any other time in the history of the Church. These Marian revelations contain concurring Gospel messages that seek to encourage the faithful to live the more challenging parts of the Gospel of Jesus Christ.

First we will look at the nature and purpose of private revelation and, in particular, Marian private revelation as understood by the Church. Secondly, we will examine the basic Marian message to the modern world by focusing on a few of the principal Marian apparitions in this Marian Age and their corresponding messages to contemporary humanity.

Nature and Purpose of Private Revelation

Public revelation is God's manifestation or revelation (Latin, *revelare*, to unveil or disclose) of divine truths for humanity's salvation, and it ends with the death of the last apostle, John. These divine truths are transmitted through Scripture and Tradition as safeguarded by the Magisterium of the Church and comprise the deposit of faith entrusted to the Church.

Private revelation constitutes a revelation given by God to an individual for the spiritual benefit of the person, a specific group or the entire Church. In contrast to public revelation, private revelation has as its God-intended purpose *not* the revelation of new doctrine, but rather to encourage and lead the faithful to *live* the revealed truths of public revelation.

Pope John XXIII refers to this purpose of authentic private revelation in his 1959 address at the close of the Marian year:

> The Roman pontiffs...if they have been constituted the guardians and interpreters of the Divine Revelation contained in Scripture and Tradition, also have the duty, when after mature examination, they deem it necessary for the common good of bringing to the attention of the faithful those supernatural lights which it pleases God to dispense freely to certain privileged souls, *not for the purpose of presenting new doctrines, but rather to guide us in our conduct* [emphasis added].[1]

The function of private revelation is to urge the faithful to return to lives committed to the divine truths of public revelation, which include the most challenging Gospel calls to generous prayer, fasting, conversion, penance and overall Christian sacrifice.

Clearly, between the Old Testament revelation to the people of Israel and the full revelation of God's Word in the person of

Jesus Christ given to the apostles, God revealed all that was necessary for the salvation of humanity. There would, therefore, be no need for later doctrinal additions through private revelation. But the challenge to live wholeheartedly the Gospel messages of continual faith, prayer, penance, conversion and spiritual peace will always remain. The value of authentic private revelation, then, is to encourage the faithful to incorporate into their lives the challenging aspects of the Gospel message or, in the words of John XXIII, to "guide us in our conduct."

Theology of Private Revelation

Theologically, private revelation is associated with the gift of prophecy (cf. 1 Cor 12:10; Rom 12:6; Eph 4:11), whereby God grants the bearer a special revelation for the common good of the Church in order to encourage the faithful to seek a more dedicated adherence to the Gospel. The reality of authentic private revelation as a result of the outpouring of the Holy Spirit is scripturally verified in the prophecy of Joel: "And it shall come to pass after this, that I will pour out my Spirit upon all flesh: and your sons and your daughters shall prophesy; your old men shall dream dreams, and *your young men shall see visions*" (Joel 2:31). Accounts of prophecy are recorded in Scripture itself (cf. Agabus, four daughters of Philip, Acts 21:9-10).

Throughout ecclesial history, numerous authentic private revelations have been recognized and approved by the Church. For example, revelations are reported in the Didache 15:1 (60-120 A.D.), the writings of Pastor Hermas 11:7 (second century), St. Gertrude (1301), St. Brigid of Sweden (1373), St. Margaret Mary Alacoque (1690), not to mention the large numbers of approved Marian apparitions throughout Church history.

St. Thomas Aquinas rightly taught that the revelation of new doctrine ended with the death of John the Apostle. But private revelation directed to guiding human action will always be present in the Church:

> At all times there have not been lacking persons having the spirit of prophecy, not indeed for the declaration of any new doctrine of faith, but for the direction of human acts.[2]

Hence, these special revelations granted by God are referred to as "private," not because they were necessarily to be limited to the knowledge of a few individuals (since their general purpose is for the upholding of the Church, sometimes local, sometimes universal), but to distinguish them from the public or official deposit of faith entrusted to and safeguarded by the Church.

Among private revelations, spiritual writers and theologians usually distinguish between three general kinds of visions: 1) "corporeal visions," or visions with a bodily appearance which are perceived by the external senses and are often called apparitions; 2) imaginative visions which are perceived by the internal sense of the imagination, either during waking hours or during sleep; 3) intellectual visions which are directly perceived by the mind, either during sleep or waking hours. Some visions can exhibit several of these characteristics at the same time. Locutions (Latin, *locutio*, speech) are supernatural words that can also be received corporally, intellectually or by the imagination. Both visions and locutions can come from a divine Person of the Trinity, the Blessed Virgin Mary, angels, saints, or even possibly demons.[3]

Response of the Church to Private Revelation

How does the Church respond to the domain of private revelation? The Church obviously acknowledges the existence of authentic private revelation by her history, but at the same time exercises a proper caution in its regard. Technically, the Church does not need private revelation in light of the Gospel, but she has always remained open to its possibility for the great fruits of encouraging the faithful to live the Gospel to its fullness.

The Church, in her wisdom, avoids the presumption of being closed to any additional graces which Christ wishes to bestow on His Church in any given historical period. At the same time, the Church does not want to risk the loss of confidence in her office as guardian of public revelation through any premature or hasty approval of a particular private revelation that may not be of supernatural origin. And so, the Church is, to use the proper expression, "open, but cautious" in response to the realm of private revelation.

Church Evaluation of Marian Apparitions

What norms or criteria does the Church use in evaluating a reported private revelation? The general criteria used by the Church in evaluating a reported Marian apparition can be divided into these three categories: 1) the revealed message content; 2) the nature of ecstasy and other concurring phenomena; 3) the spiritual fruits.[4]

Any reported message revealed in a private revelation must be examined in light of the public revelation contained in Scripture and Tradition as safeguarded by the Church. If any reported message conveys a substantial doctrinal or moral error against Church teaching, the reported revelations are deemed to be false. For the Holy Spirit, the same divine source of inspiration for public revelation and authentic private revelation alike, cannot contradict Himself. Since private revelation is at the service of public revelation, then the "command to act" given by private revelation must correspond to the "revealed doctrine" of public revelation.

Secondly, the nature of ecstasy experienced by the "visionary" or recipient of prophecy or apparition is another principal factor in the process of Church investigation. Oftentimes, the visionary or recipient of a major private revelation is partially removed from an ordinary time and space experience during the God-granted revelation, and is partially brought into the temporal-spatial experience of the giver of the revelation, whether it be Jesus or Mary. In other words, the visionary is brought into an ecstatic state that at least partially transcends his usual sense experience.

A medieval means of testing the authenticity of a reported visionary during ecstasy included the injecting of a large needle into the arm of the alleged visionary to test the legitimacy of his or her ecstatic state. The much improved modern means of medico-scientific testing during a reported ecstasy (which includes EKG, EEG, and other technoligical data) has been a great help to the Church in distinguishing empirically a legitimate state of ecstasy from a false report.[5]

Other phenomena related to private revelation and worthy of examination include reported physical signs, such as solar miracles (as at Fatima), or miraculous springs (as at Lourdes), which cannot be explained by natural means, but only by a direct intervention of God.

Thirdly, the spiritual fruits constitute a major criterion for the authenticity of a private revelation, based on the scriptural message in which Our Lord refers to the good tree bearing good fruit: "for the tree is known by its fruit" (Mt 12:33). One of the best indications for the authenticity of a reported private revelation is when the resulting devotion manifests true and ongoing conversion, as seen in a return to the prayer and sacramental life of the Church (i.e., Mass, Confession, Rosary, fraternal charity, etc.).

Although it is possible for some spiritual fruits to result

temporarily from a false private revelation because of its partial conveyance of the truths of Christianity; nonetheless, a revelation of either human or satanic origin cannot manifest substantial and consistent spiritual fruits comparable to the qualitative and quantitative spiritual benefits of a true revelation which has God as its ultimate source. The work of God and the work of man or Satan can never be seen as having identical fruits.

It is also noteworthy that even in the case of an authentic private revelation, it often happens that some error in the receiving or the transmitting of the revelation may occur because of the ever present human nature of the visionary. Several authentic private revelations that have received official Church approval have also had some secondary elements of human error, even when the visionary has been a canonized saint.[6]

If, after proper examination (usually performed at the diocesan level by the local bishop), the Church is satisfied with the indications of authenticity and has excluded probabilities of error or fraud, she can grant her official approval. Normally, official Church approval means that there is nothing against faith and morals in the revelation and concurring phenomena, and that the faithful are free to accept the private revelation without concern for doctrinal or moral error. This is sometimes called a "negative approval," meaning the Church does not guarantee its authenticity, but officially pronounces the revelation free from doctrinal or moral error and thereby worthy of belief. This doctrinal clearance allows the faithful greater freedom regarding the acceptance of the revelation.

Degrees of Church Approval

Historically, the Church has exercised different degrees of official approval in regard to Marian private revelations. For example, to the Marian apparitions at Knock, Ireland (1879), the Church gave what may be called an "approval by omission." By withholding official judgment and examining the devotion that came as a result of the reported apparitions, the Church has indirectly approved Knock as authentic by the acknowledgements of "Our Lady of Knock" and by visits to the apparition from Church authorities (for example, by Pope John Paul II).

Other reported Marian apparitions have received a degree of Church approval that goes beyond the usual negative approval, i.e., that it is not contrary to faith and morals. A few apparitions have actually received a positive judgment concerning their authenticity from the local bishop. This has happened, for example, in the Marian apparitions at Beauraing, Belgium in 1932-33, and in Bethania, Venezuela in 1987.

Any degree of official Church approval does not oblige the faithful to accept a Marian revelation, since it never directly affects the public revelation contained in the deposit of faith. Authentic private revelation, therefore, is normally given the assent of "human faith" based on prudential discernment, but not "divine faith" appropriate for public revelation.

As Pope Benedict XIV stated:

Even though many of these revelations have been approved, we cannot and ought not give them the assent of divine faith, but only that of human faith, according to the dictates of prudence whenever these dictates enable us to decide that they are probable and worthy of pious credence.[7]

On the other hand, the fact that the Church has given her approval after careful and oftentimes scrutinous examination offers strong moral evidence for the prudence of human acceptance of a particular revelation. This is specifically the case regarding private revelations that the Church has "made her own" through papal statements, visits, and even liturgical celebrations, such as has happened with the revelations of the Sacred Heart of Jesus to St. Margaret Alacoque or the Marian apparitions of Lourdes and Fatima.

Moreover, it would be reprehensible if any Catholic, after the Church had granted her negative approval of a private revelation, were to contradict or ridicule a Church-approved private revelation or its corresponding devotion. Although the general faithful are called to give only an assent of human faith, it is also theologically held that the visionary and any others intimately connected with the revelation may and should accept the revelation with the assent of divine faith.[8]

Marian Message to the Modern World

The present era of the Church rightfully deserves the designation of the Age of Mary with its unequalled reception of Marian apparitions. This extraordinary number of Marian visits should evoke from the faithful a gratitude to God for this time of extraordinary graces. But it should also evoke a serious realism, a balanced reading of the signs of the times, about the needy state of the world that necessitates such an exceptional number of heavenly visits from humanity's Spiritual Mother.

What constitutes the overall Marian message to the modern world? We will try to summarize the heart of the Marian message to the modern world by briefly examining the revealed messages from a few of the most universal Marian apparitions that have occured in the last two centuries.

Miraculous Medal Revelation

The beginning of the Marian Era may be assigned to the Marian revelation of the Miraculous Medal in 1830. A Marian vision was granted to St. Catherine Labouré, a religious sister of the Daughters of Charity. At the Paris motherhouse on November 27, 1830, the Blessed Virgin appeared standing upon a globe and crushing a serpent beneath her feet (cf. Gen 3:15). Rays of light, symbolizing graces from the Mediatrix, streamed from her outstretched hands. Around the image of Mary the following prayer was written: "O Mary, conceived without sin, pray for us who have recourse to thee."

The vision was then turned around, revealing a cross linked to an "M" by a horizontal bar through the top of the "M." Beneath the letter "M" were the Hearts of Jesus and Mary, the former crowned with thorns and the latter pierced with a sword (cf. Lk 2:35). The entire image was also encircled with twelve stars (cf. Rev 12:1).

During the vision, Mary instructed St. Catherine with the following words: "Have a medal struck after this model. All who wear it will receive great graces. They should wear it around the neck."

The Archbishop of Paris granted permission for the first medals to be struck in 1832. So many spiritual and physical benefits were received upon the promulgation of the medal that people termed the medal "miraculous," and hence its present name. A Church investigation in 1836 approved its supernatural authenticity, and specific papal approval of its devotion was granted in 1842. Since the time of its origin, the devout wearing of the Miraculous Medal has spread throughout the Catholic world. Those who wear the medal have received blessings and indulgences from many popes, including Pius IX, Leo XIII, Pius X, Pius XI, Pius XII, John XXIII, and Paul VI.

The Miraculous Medal revelation was said to have given positive encouragement to Pope Pius IX for the infallible definition of Mary's Immaculate Conception, based on the revealed words: "O Mary, *conceived without sin*, pray for us who have recourse to thee."

The Miraculous Medal devotion continues to flourish today with an endless list of spiritual benefits for those who wear the medal faithfully as a sign of their devotion and love of the Immaculate Mother of God.[9]

The Message of Lourdes

In 1858 the Blessed Virgin Mary appeared to Bernadette Soubirous (age 14) in the small mountain town of Lourdes, France. Between February 11 and July 16, 1858 Bernadette received eighteen apparitions of the Blessed Virgin. The message of Mary in this early stage of the Marian Era is one of prayer and penance in reparation to God and for the conversion of sinners.

In the sixth apparition Mary said to Bernadette: "Pray for the sinners." In the eighth apparition, Mary communicated to Bernadette: "You must pray to God for sinners." Bernadette reported the words: "Penitence, Penitence, Penitence."

Throughout the apparitions at Lourdes, there is the call to pray the Rosary, primarily through the example of Mary herself. During all the apparitions, Mary was praying the Rosary silently, moving the beads through her fingers. Bernadette also felt an interior impulse to pray the Rosary. At the beginning and end of each apparition the Rosary was prayed by Bernadette and the surrounding peoples.

In the ninth apparition, Mary directed Bernadette to uncover the physical sign of a miraculous spring. The following is Bernadette's account of the event:

While I was in prayer, the Lady said to me in a friendly, but serious voice, "Go, drink and wash in the spring." As I did not know where this spring was, and as I did not think the matter important, I went towards the river. The Lady called me back and signed to me with her finger to go under the grotto to the left; I obeyed but I did not see any water. Not knowing where to get it from, I scratched the earth and the water came. I let it get a little clear of the mud, then I drank and washed.[10]

The physical spring at Lourdes has resulted in several documented miracles and is a Marian precedent for a consistent presence of physical signs at the apparition sites. These physical signs are meant to encourage the faithful to accept and to live out her Gospel messages.

During the eleventh apparition, the Lady requested the construction of a chapel at the apparition site: "Go and tell the priests that a chapel must be built here."

During the sixteenth apparition, we have a profound self-revelation of Mary confirming the infallible statement of Pope Pius IX some four years earlier. Bernadette tells us:

"When I was on my knees before the Lady," she continued, "I asked her pardon for arriving late. Always good and gracious, she made a sign to me with her head that I need not excuse myself. Then I spoke to her of all my affection, all my respect and the happiness I had in seeing her again. After having poured out my heart to her I took up my Rosary. While I was praying, the thought of asking her name came before my mind with such persistence that I could think of nothing else. I feared to be presumptuous in repeating a question she had always refused to answer. And yet something compelled me to speak. At last, under an irresistible impulse, the words fell from my mouth, and I begged the Lady to tell me who she was. The Lady did as she had always done before; she bowed her head and smiled but she did not reply. I cannot say why, but I felt myself bolder and asked her again to graciously tell me her name; however she only bowed and smiled as before, still remaining silent. Then once more, for a third time, clasping my hands and confessing myself unworthy of the favour I was asking of her, I again made my request.... The Lady was standing above the rose-bush, in a position very similar to that shown in the miraculous medal. At the third request her face became very serious and she seemed to bow down in an attitude of humility. Then she joined her hands and raised them to her breast.... She looked up to Heaven...then slowly opening her hands and leaning forward towards me, she said to me in a voice vibrating with emotion: *'I am the Immaculate Conception'*!"

We see in this apparition not only the confirmation of dogma but a personal revelation from the Blessed Virgin herself.

In sum, the message of Lourdes is a general Marian call to penance and prayer, particularly the Rosary, for the conversion of sinners and in reparation to God.

The Message of Fatima

The 1917 Marian apparitions at Fatima continue the basic Marian message to the modern world, but with greater specificity and concretization. Along with the general call to prayer and penance, Mary, under the title of "Our Lady of the Rosary," added these specific requests at Fatima: the daily praying of the Rosary; the offering of daily sacrifices to God; and devotion to her Immaculate Heart (which includes the Five First Saturdays of Reparation).

The apparitions of Fatima were prefaced by three 1916 angelic apparitions to three Portuguese children: Lucia (age 10), Jacinta (age 7) and Francesco (age 8). Historically, the Fatima apparitions concurred with the climax of World War I.

The most informative of the 1917 apparitions of Fatima was the third apparition of July 13. This apparition contained a vision of hell; a call to devotion to Mary's Immaculate Heart; and a prediction of things to come (including the Second World War) if people did not respond by praying the daily Rosary. From Lucia's Memoirs, we read:

A few moments after arriving at the Cova da Iria, near the holmoak, where a large number of people were praying the Rosary, we saw the flash of light once more, and a moment later Our Lady appeared on the holmoak.

"What do you want of me?" I [Lucia] asked.

"I want you to come here on the 13th of next month, to continue to pray the Rosary every day in honour of Our Lady of the Rosary, in order to obtain peace for the world and the end of the war, because only she can help you...."

"Sacrifice yourselves for sinners, and say many times, especially whenever you make some sacrifice: O Jesus, it is for love of You, for the conversion of sinners, and in reparation for the sins committed against the Immaculate Heart of Mary."

As Our Lady spoke these last words, she opened her hands once more, as she had done during the two previous months. The rays of light seemed to penetrate the earth, and we saw, as it were, a sea of fire. Plunged in this fire were demons and souls in human form, like transparent burning embers, all blackened or burnished bronze, floating about in the conflagration, now raised into the air by the flames that issued from within themselves together with great clouds of smoke, now falling back on every side like sparks in huge fires, without weight or equilibrium, amid shrieks and groans of pain and despair, which horrified us and made us tremble with fear. (It must have been this sight which caused me to cry out, as people say they heard me.) The demons could be distinguished by their terrifying and repellent likeness to frightful and unknown animals, black and transparent like burning coals. Terrified and as if to plead for succour, we looked up at Our Lady, who said to us, so kindly and sadly:

"You have seen hell where the souls of poor sinners go. To save them, God wishes to establish in the world devotion to my Immaculate Heart. If what I say to you is done, many souls will be saved and there will be peace. The war is going to end; but if people do not cease offending God, a worse one will break out during the pontificate of Pius XI. When you see a night illuminated by an unknown light, know that this is the great sign given you by God that he is about to punish the world for its crimes, by means of war, famine, and persecutions of the Church and the Holy Father.

"To prevent this, I shall come to ask for the consecration of Russia to my Immaculate Heart, and the Communion of Reparation on the First Saturdays. If my requests are heeded, Russia will be converted, and there will be peace; if not, she will spread her errors throughout the world, causing wars and persecutions of the Church. The good will be martyred, the Holy Father will have much to suffer, various nations will be annihilated. In the end, my Immaculate Heart will triumph. The Holy Father will consecrate Russia to me, and she will be converted, and a period of peace will be granted to the world. In

Portugal, the dogma of the Faith will always be preserved...

"When you pray the Rosary, say after each mystery: O my Jesus, forgive us, save us from the fire of hell. Lead all souls to Heaven, especially those who are most in need."[11]

This third Fatima message introduced the title "Our Lady of the Rosary" and re-emphasized the crucial need to pray the Rosary daily for world peace and for the end of World War I—a goal that could be obtained only through the intercession of Mary.

The three Portuguese children then received a vision confirming the reality of Hell and a prophecy of a Second World War, persecutions of the Church, the annihilation of nations and suffering by the Pope because of the ubiquitous offenses against God.

But Our Lady of the Rosary also revealed a message of hope. Through the consecration of Russia to her Immaculate Heart and the later revealed First Saturdays of Reparation, Mary's Immaculate Heart will triumph in the end and a period of peace will be granted to the world.

In the final 1917 apparition on October 13, Mary identified herself as Our Lady of the Rosary and again called the world to pray the Rosary daily for peace in the world. The following is from Lucia's account:

"I want to tell you that a chapel is to be built here in my honour. I am the Lady of the Rosary. Continue always to pray the Rosary every day. The war is going to end, and the soldiers will soon return to their homes."

"I have many things to ask you: the cure of some sick

persons, the conversion of sinners and other things...."

"Some yes, but not others. They must amend their lives and ask forgiveness for their sins."

Looking very sad, Our Lady said:

"Do not offend the Lord our God any more, because He is already so much offended."

Then, opening her hands, she made them reflect on the sun, and she ascended, the reflection of her own light continued to be projected on the sun itself....

After Our Lady had disappeared into the immense distance of the firmament, we beheld St. Joseph with the Child Jesus and Our Lady robed in white with a blue mantle, beside the sun. St. Joseph and the Child Jesus appeared to bless the world, for they traced the Sign of the Cross with their hands. When, a little later, this apparition disappeared, I saw Our Lord and Our Lady; it seemed to me that it was Our Lady of Dolours. Our Lord appeared to bless the world in the same manner as St. Joseph had done. This apparition also vanished, and I saw Our Lady once more, this time resembling Our Lady of Carmel.

Following this sixth apparition the seventy thousand on-lookers reported seeing the physical sign of the solar miracle. The sun appeared to dance in the sky, giving off various colors and then approached the earth with great intensity, only to return later to its position in the sky.

The seventh apparition to the professed Sr. Lucia of the Immaculate Heart took place in the Spanish convent on

December 10, 1925. It is here that the revelation of the Five First Saturday devotions took place. This is the account from Lucia's diary:

On December 10, 1925, the most Holy Virgin appeared to her, and by her side, elevated by a luminous cloud, was a child. The most holy Virgin rested her hand on her shoulder, and as she did so, she showed her a heart encircled by thorns, which she was holding in her hand. At the same time, the Child said:

"Have compassion on the Heart of your most holy Mother, covered with thorns, with which ungrateful men pierce it at every moment, and there is no one to make an act of reparation to remove them."

Then the most holy Virgin said:

"Look, my daughter, at my Heart, surrounded with thorns with which ungrateful men pierce me at every moment by their blasphemies and ingratitude. You at least try to console me, and say that I promise to assist at the hour of death, with the graces necessary for salvation, all those who, on the first Saturday of five consecutive months, shall confess, receive Holy Communion, recite five decades of the Rosary, and keep me company for fifteen minutes while meditating on the fifteen mysteries of the Rosary, with the intention of making reparation to me."

We see here in the same spirit as the Scapular devotion, the efforts of the Mother of Jesus to intercede for salvation based on the response of the faithful. The great gift of the Five First Saturdays has a strong sacramental call at its base with Eucharistic devotion and the reception of the sacrament of Confession. It also relays another spiritual incentive to praying and meditating on the Rosary.

In sum, the message of Fatima, continues the same Marian message to the modern world seen at Lourdes, but with further specificity in terms of the daily praying of the Rosary, the offering of sacrifices to God in reparation to the Heart of Mary, and the Five First Saturdays devotion.

Contemporary Reported Apparitions

Since the time of the Second Vatican Council, an unprecedented number of Marian apparitions have been reported throughout the world. Marian apparitions have been reported from such international locations as Nicaragua; Akita, Japan; Medjugorje, Bosnia-Hercegovina; Kibeho, Africa; NaJu, Korea; Bethania, Venezuela; Hrushiv, Ukraine; and several other places. A good number of these apparitions have received official approval, while others still remain under Church investigation.

How should the faithful respond to a reported apparition before the Church has granted her official approval? The faithful are free to believe in a reported apparition if nothing in the message or concurring phenomena are contrary to faith and morals as taught by the Church.

It is precisely the response of the faithful to a reported apparition site that invites the Church authorities to enter into a process of official evaluation and examination—a process which is of upmost value to the faithful. Any individual determination concerning a reported Marian apparition must include a clear willingness to accept in obedience the final and definitive judgment of the Church.

For example, when the seventy thousand onlookers at Fatima saw the solar miracle and began along with the visionaries to live the *message* of Fatima in 1917, before official Church approval was given in 1930, they were in no sense violating proper Catholic response to private revelation or Church authority. It is an historical fact that the Basilica at Fatima was well under construction and the hospital completed by the time the 1930 official approval by the Church was pronounced. Nonetheless, before an announcement is made regarding any reported Marian revelation, the Christian must retain an attitude of obedience to the final and definitive judgment of the Church.

The Message of Medjugorje [12]

Of the various contemporary reported Marian apparitions, none has received more international response from the faithful throughout the world than those coming from a small Bosnian mountain town known as "Medjugorje" (which means, "between the hills").

Although still under Church investigation, the reported Marian apparitions from Medjugorje have received strong unofficial endorsement from the vast majority of bishops, theologians, mariologists, priests, scientists, doctors and faithful who have investigated the Medjugorje event in light of authentic Church criteria.

Let us examine the basic message of the reported Medjugorje apparitions as an example of a contemporary Marian apparition that fits well into the overall content and development of the Marian message to the modern world.

The basic message of Mary under the title, "Queen of Peace," to six Croatian youths beginning on June 24, 1981 (and reportedly continuing at the time of this work), can be summarized under five themes: Faith, Prayer, Fasting, Conversion and Peace.

The theme of faith is a Marian call for a more committed

faith in the one God and in Jesus Christ as the one Mediator to the Father.

The Medjugorje call to prayer constitutes a greater generosity in terms of both quality and quantity of prayer, summarized in the often used request for "prayer of the heart." Apart from the invitation to daily Mass and Eucharistic adoration, the Blessed Virgin has asked for the daily praying of the fifteen decade Rosary, the frequent reading of Scripture and a personal consecration of all peoples to the Sacred Heart of Jesus and the Immaculate Heart of Mary. Several of the monthly messages (given on the 25th of each month) echo the simple but persevering refrain: "Pray! Pray! Pray!"

The Medjugorje call for fasting began with a call to fast on Fridays, and in August 1984, the Blessed Virgin requested that Wednesdays also be added as a day of strict fasting. This Wednesday and Friday fasting practice reflects the same practice present in the first centuries of the Church, as recorded in the Didache (c. 60-120 A.D.): "Do not fast like the hypocrites on Monday and Thursday; you [Christians] are to fast on Wednesday and Friday."[13] Rather than requesting a new fasting practice, it appears that the Blessed Virgin seeks to return the faithful to the more committed fasting practice of the early Church.

The conversion theme from the Madonna, as she is referred to, is a theme of greater conversion to Jesus Christ, specifically through the reception of the Sacrament of Reconciliation at least on a monthly basis. On the third day of her apparitions, June 26, 1981, she transmitted the following message: "Peace, peace, peace, nothing but peace. Men must be reconciled with God and with one another. For this to happen, it is necessary to believe, to pray, to fast and to go to Confession."

Lastly from Medjugorje, the theme of peace calls for the spiritual peace of Christ in the heart of each believer as the fruit of greater prayer, greater faith, greater fasting and greater conversion. This interior spiritual peace of Christ in the heart should then blossom to family peace, social peace with the eventual goal of world peace. But a global peace is possible only if it is founded upon the spiritual and interior peace of Jesus Christ in the hearts of humanity.

Also present in the Medjugorje message is the reference to a conditional world chastisement (similar to the message of Fatima) if the human race does not repent and turn from its ubiquitous sin. Nonetheless, the overriding theme of spiritual peace remains the heart of the Medjugorje message as confirmed in Mary's title as Queen of Peace.[14]

In sum, the message of Medjugorje seems to represent the full flowering of the consistent Marian message to the modern world: a greater generosity in prayer (especially the Rosary), penance, and the Church's sacramental life (Mass and Confession) offered to God in reparation for sin and the conversion of the world. Again it must be said regarding any reported Marian private revelation that the faithful are free to accept or reject the reported apparition based on the individual's investigation, but must retain an attitude of full and complete obedience to the final and definitive judgment of the Church. For the Church's Magisterium is and always will be the final authority over both Public Revelation and Private Revelation alike.

In sum we can say that, although they are not necessary as an element of public revelation contained in the Church's deposit of faith, the many appearances of the Mother of Jesus to humanity in this Age of Mary have been nothing short of an inestimable gift to the Church and has very probably led to the salvation and sanctification of many who otherwise would have neglected the living of the full Gospel of Our Lord, Jesus Christ.

We conclude with the words of the theologian Garrigou-LaGrange, O.P. who, as far back as the 1930's, spoke strongly of the need for responding to the Marian message to the modern world:

Exterior peace will not be obtained for the world except by the interior peace of souls, bringing them back to God and working to establish the reign of Christ in the depths of their intellects, of their hearts, and of their wills. For this return of straying souls to Him Who alone can save them, it is necessary to have recourse to the intercession of Mary, Universal Mediatrix and Mother of all men. It is said of sinners who seem forever lost that they must be confided to Mary: it is the same for Christian peoples who stray. All the influence of the Blessed Virgin has its end to lead them to her Son....

That is why on all sides many interior souls, before the unprecedented disorders and tragic sufferings of the hour, feel the need for recourse to the redeeming love of Christ through the intercession of Mary Mediatrix.[15]

Notes

1. Pope John XXIII, closing statement of 1959 Marian year, February 18, 1959.
2. St. Thomas Aquinas, *Summa Theologica*, II-II, Q. 174, art. 6, ad 3.
3. Cf. St. John of the Cross, *The Ascent of Mount Carmel*, Bk II; G.M. Roschini, O.S.M., *The Virgin Mary in the Writings of Maria Valtorta* (Quebec: Kolbe Publications, 1989) p. 10, footnote 9.
4. For discussion of Church criteria, cf. R. Laurentin, "Role of Apparitions in the Life of the Church," presentation at National Conference on Medjugorje, Notre Dame University, May 12, 1989.
5. For example, cf. R. Laurentin and H. Joyeux, *Scientific and Medical Studies in the Apparitions at Medjugorje*, (Dublin: Veritas Press, 1987).
6. Cf. Augustin Paulan, *Graces of Interior Prayer*, St. Louis, 1950.
7. Pope Benedict XIV, *De servorum Dei beatificatione et beatorum canonizatione*, v. 1-7 of Opera Omnia, 17 v. in 20; 2:32; 3:53.
8. Cf. Jordan Aumann, O.P. *Spiritual Theology*, (London: Sheed and Ward) p. 429.
9. Cf. Delaney, *A Woman Clothed With the Sun*, (New York: Doubleday) 1961. "Miraculous Medal," New Catholic Encyclopedia, Vol. 13, 1978.
10. This quote and all other quotes of Bernadette Soubirous and accounts of Lourdes taken from J.B. Estrade, J.H. Girolestone, tr., *The Appearance of the Blessed Virgin Mary at the Grotto of Lourdes*, (Westminster: Art and Book Co., Ltd., 1912); cf. also Alan Heame, *The Happenings at Lourdes* (London: Catholic Book Club, 1968).
11. This quote and all other quotes from Lucia and the account of Fatima taken from *Fatima in Lucia's Own Words: Sister Lucia's Memoirs*, ed. Kondar, SVD, Postulation Center, distributed by Our Blessed Lady of Victory Mission, Brookings, South Dakota, 1976.
12. Medjugorje message is a summary from M. Miravalle, *The Message of Medjugorje: The Marian Message to the Modern World* (Lanham, Maryland: University Press of America, 1986).
13. Didache 8:1, Glimm, tr., *Fathers of the Church* (New York: C.I.M.A., 1947) I, p.177.
14. For a more basic summary of the Medjugorje message cf. M. Miravalle, *Heart of the Message of Medjugorje* (Steubenville, Ohio: Franciscan University Press, 1988).
15. Garrigou-LaGrange, O.P., *Mother of the Saviour and the Interior Life*, p.317.

chapter seven

In Defense of Mary: Responding to Objections

In God's perfect providence, the Mother of Jesus is intended to be an instrument and symbol of profound unity. For along with the unity in grace that comes from sharing in the grace of Jesus Christ as our Brother, the Father also intended the universal (catholic) unity of all members of the human family by calling one woman, "Mother." And yet, because of her roles of being both Mother of God and Mother of the Church in its fullness, Mary has been perceived as an occasion for division.

Nothing breaks the heart of a mother more than division among her children, especially when she herself is posed as one of the principal reasons for the disunity! But in truth, Mary in her doctrine and devotion is a cause for division only when she reflects her Son, the sign of contradiction to the world (cf. Lk 2:34), and the Body of her Son, the Church, which has been entrusted with safeguarding the revelation of Christ without compromise until He comes again in glory.

Although it is not the intent of this particular work to give a comprehensive response to every objection of the role of the Blessed Virgin Mary, nor is there space, we would like to offer a basic response to ten of the more common objections to points of Marian doctrine and devotion.

General Objections

OBJECTION 1: Objection to "Mariolatry"

Objection: Catholics worship Mary in a manner that violates the First Commandment, offering adoration to her through her images and statues; an adoration due to God alone.

Response: As discussed in the first chapter, a distinction must be made between adoration (*latria*) and veneration (*dulia*). The Church has never taught that acts of adoration, the reverence and glory due to God alone, are to be given to Mary, but only an exceptional veneration (*hyperdulia*) because of her unique association with Jesus Christ in His work of redeeming humanity.

We must avoid misunderstandings that can arise through the use of the term "worship." Traditionally, as was mentioned, "worship" has been used for both adoration and veneration, and the word itself simply indicates a worthiness of some type of honor or dignity (from the Old English, *weorthscipe*). Although prudence may encourage reserving the term worship exclusively for adoration because of the potential misunderstandings of today, the classical use of the term refers to a broader kind of honor and, hence, cannot be viewed as an example of giving adoration to Mary when the expression "worship of Mary" is used.

In regards to the "worshipping" of Marian statues and images, again we must distinguish. First of all, within the authentic Catholic Church there is no adoration given to Marian images (an act mistakenly perceived to model the pagan worship of idols). A painting or a statue of Mary serves the same purpose as a family photo on an office desk, or a statue of a public hero or statesman erected in a town square. The image serves as a reminder of the person the image represents, and thereby possesses a symbolic or representational value, not a true personal value in itself.

As the father gazes upon the photograph of his family on his desk at work and feels the warming of his heart at the thought of his wife and children, so too, an image of Jesus' Mother can evoke similar feelings of filial love and devotion to her. But, as is true of the family photo and the public memorial statue, the Marian statue or image possesses no intrinsic power nor personhood; it only conveys an image of a heavenly Spiritual Mother most deserving of our earthly devotion and love.

OBJECTION 2: Objection Against Scriptural Bases of Marian Doctrine

Objection: How can Catholics accept Marian doctrines like the Immaculate Conception and the Assumption when they are not explicitly revealed in the Bible?

Response: This question implies a certain misunderstanding about the sources of Divine Revelation, as discussed in the Introduction. The idea that all divinely revealed truths are explicitly contained in Scripture, is, in short, "unscriptural." Some will quote the Scripture passage of 2 Tim 3:16 to support the position known as *sola scriptura* (Scripture alone): "Everything in the scripture has been divinely inspired, and it has its uses: to instruct us, to expose our errors, to correct our faults, to educate in holy living."

While this inspired passage describes the great fruits of Sacred Scripture, it nowhere even infers that Scripture is the only source of revelation. In fact, John Henry Newman, in his writing, *Inspiration in its Relation to Revelation*, explains: "This passage furnishes no argument whatever that the Sacred Scripture, without Tradition, is the *sole rule of faith*; for although Sacred Scripture is *profitable* for these four ends, still it is not said to be sufficient. The Apostle [Paul] requires the aid of Tradition" (2 Thes 2:15).[1]

Moreover, it is explicitly taught in Scripture that the Bible is *not* the only source of Divine Revelation. The last Gospel ends with St. John telling us that everything Christ said and did is not recorded in Scripture (Jn 21:25), and St. Paul attests to much Christian teaching being handed down in the oral tradition of the Church (2 Thes 2:2).

Historically, one must remember that for the first decades of the Church, there were no New Testament writings (since the first estimated New Testament writing was St. Paul's Letter to the Thessalonians in approximately 51 A.D.). But there was the oral tradition of the Church which handed down the saving Gospel and doctrine of Jesus Christ (cf. Acts 2:42; 2 Thes 2:15).

Therefore, the proper question that should be asked regarding Marian doctrine is: "Can these Marian truths be found in the full sources of Divine Revelation, Sacred Scripture and Sacred Tradition, as safeguarded by the Magisterium? To this question, one can answer an emphatic "yes." For every Marian doctrine, we have at least implicit (and some explicit) Scripture references containing the revealed seed of the doctrine (i.e., the Immaculate Conception [Gen 3:15, Lk 1:28]; the Assumption [Gen 3:15; Ps 131:8; Rev 11:19; Rev 12:1]); copious references from Sacred Tradition, and the *de fide* teachings of the Church's Magisterium, including explicit papal infallible definitions (see Chapter 2, "The Person of Mary in Doctrine").

Objections to Marian Doctrines

OBJECTION 3: Objection to Mary as Intercessor and Spiritual Mother

Objection: Mary's role as intercessor and Spiritual Mother assumes an ability of Mary, and of the saints in general, to intercede from Heaven, which presupposes the complete knowledge and power of God Himself, and this in itself is not scriptural.

Response: The right and appropriateness both to venerate the saints and to seek their intercession are expressly taught by the Church (Council of Trent, D986, 984, 998 and Vatican II, *Lumen Gentium,* No. 51) and can be deduced from scriptural revelation, as in the case of the veneration of the angels (cf. Jos 5:14; Dn 33:2; Tob 12:16).

The angels have a supernatural dignity worthy of honor which comes from their intimate union with God (cf. Mt 18:10). Since the saints are also intimately united with God (1 Cor 13:12; 1 Jn 3:2), then they also deserve our honor and veneration (see Chapter 1 on *dulia*).

The Jewish people manifested faith in the intercession of saints as attested to by Judas the Maccabean (2 Mac 15:11-16), and in the ability of the angels and saints to offer prayers at the feet of God and support them with their intercession (cf. Tob 12:12; Rev 5:8, 8:3).

St. Paul asked for prayerful intercession from many other disciples (Rom 15:30; Col 4:3; 1 Thes 5:25) and also referred to his prayers for them (2 Thes 1:11). And since Heaven is a state of God's living saints (Mk 12:26-27), St. Paul can certainly continue his prayers for his fellow members of the Body of Christ.

Only a misconception about Heaven as a stagnant, isolated part of the Body of Christ, an assembly without concern or love for the rest of the Body still seeking the crown of heavenly glory, would lead to the conclusion that the saints do not continue their prayer and intercession for their beloved family on earth.

And since Mary is Mother of the Head and of the Body, her

maternal intercession rightfully has an exalted ability to bring her earthly children closer to Jesus Christ. We see scripturally that Mary's intercession starts on earth with the wedding of Cana (Jn 2).

As for the need of having God's complete knowledge and power to hear prayers of the faithful on earth and to intercede, we must distinguish between having a divine nature and merely participating in providential acts through the power of God.

As is the case with the life of sanctifying grace in general, God allows creatures to participate in aspects of His life, knowledge, and power, without the creature being God Himself. The saints in Heaven do not have the restrictions of time and space which we experience on earth, but participate in God's experience of events as "one great eternal present."

The saints, therefore, have the privilege of being able to communicate with the faithful on earth, to hear our prayers and intercede on our behalf—all without being "gods," but by sharing in God's experience of reality. This is not so difficult to accept if we remember that the human ability to communicate intellectually and to pray for one another is also performed by the power of God's gifts of reason and grace.

Once again, Mary, being the Spiritual Mother of all humanity (Jn 19:26), would have a particular sharing in the one mediation of Jesus Christ (1 Tim 2:5) for the spiritual benefit of the human family. As Vatican II describes: "Taken up to heaven, she did not lay aside this saving office but by her manifold intercession continues to bring us the gifts of eternal salvation" (*Lumen Gentium*, No. 62).

OBJECTION 4: Objection Against the Immaculate Conception

Objection: How could Mary be immaculately conceived and

remain sinless throughout her earthly life when St. Paul says, "all have sinned and fall short of the glory of Christ" (Rom 3:23)? Therefore all people need a savior and redeemer, including Mary.

Response: In regards to Mary's need for a redeemer, the Church wholeheartedly agrees. As we discussed in Chapter 2 concerning the doctrine of the Immaculate Conception, Mary was redeemed by Christ precisely through her Immaculate Conception. Mary's reception of sanctifying grace at conception was an application of the graces merited by Jesus Christ on the Cross, and applied by God who, by nature, is out of time.

Mary's conception in sanctifying grace was a unique form of redemption, in fact a higher form of redemption, since through the merits of her Son she never had to receive a fallen human nature. Hence, Mary needed to be redeemed and was redeemed through a "preservative redemption," a redemption brought about through the merits of her Son on Calvary and applied to her at the moment of her conception.

This unique act of God made Mary the fitting Mother of the Word made flesh, giving Him an immaculate human nature in a fully maternal way, and meriting the title given to her by Gabriel, "full of grace" (Lk 1:28).

As to the words of St. Paul that "all have sinned" (Rom 3:23), the Church rightfully interprets this passage as a divinely revealed truth about the general masses that make up humanity. But since the teachings of St. Paul were primarily directed to spreading the Good News which had to precede an accurate understanding of Marian doctrine (Mary is who she is because of her Son), then clearly it would be inappropriate for St. Paul to make an explicit, exceptional clause about the Mother of Jesus in his teaching of the universal need for Redemption. This would be inappropriate before the people of the time had fundamental, doctrinal clarity about the basic message of the Gospel.

Clearly, St. Paul's intention in this passage of Romans was not a teaching on Marian doctrine, but a general instruction on the universal sin of humanity, and thereby the universal need for a redeemer.

Also, St. Paul's statement that "all have sinned" does not include infants before the age of reason who are incapable of sinning (since the children cannot yet choose in reason and freedom). The statement of St. Paul need not be all-inclusive to convey the divine truth that the sinning masses have unquestionable need for Our Lord, the one Redeemer of the world.

OBJECTION 5: Objection Against the Perpetual Virginity of Mary

Objection: Mary could not have remained virginal after the birth of Christ for several reasons: a) because there are scriptural references to the "brethren of the Lord" (Mt 12:46; Mk 3:31; Lk 8:19); b) because it would negate the true marriage between Mary and Joseph if it were never consummated; c) because Scripture speaks of Mary being found with child *before* she and Joseph came together: "When his mother Mary was espoused to Joseph, *before* they came together, she was found with child" (Mt 1:18), which infers that they "came together" after the birth of Jesus; and d) Scripture says Jesus was the first-born Son of Mary (Lk 2:7; Mt 1:25), which infers that additional children were born later.

Response: a) As explained in Chapter 2, the Greek word for brother, "adelphos," is often used in the Bible to mean brother, cousin, or near relative. In fact, there are several instances in the Bible where the word "adelphos" is used and, by examining the context, we know that it could not possibly refer to a relation of biological brother.

For example, in Genesis 13:8, Lot is called Abraham's "brother" ("adelphos"), although Lot was Abraham's cousin (Gen 12:5). In Genesis 29:15, Jacob is referred to as the "brother" ("adelphos") of Laban, although Jacob was actually Laban's nephew (Gen 29:10).

Hence the term "brothers of the Lord" could refer to Jesus' cousins, His near relatives, or even His disciples, as Christians today refer to themselves as "brothers and sisters of the Lord." The term "brothers of the Lord" does not create a valid scriptural objection to Mary's perpetual virginity.

b) The perpetual virginity of Mary does not constitute an impediment to a true marriage between Mary and Joseph. The essence of marriage consists in the vow of a total gift to other which includes the marital right of conjugal relations. The validity of the marriage bond lies not in the exercise of this right, but rather, in the true gift of self to the spouse. To agree mutually to offer even the material exercise of the marital rights of relations as a gift to God does not violate or prevent the essence of an authentic and valid marriage vow.

Therefore, Mary and Joseph experienced a true marriage with the total gift of self to other, even though they did not exercise the marital gift of conjugal relations.

c) The biblical words "before" and "until" state merely what has not yet taken place; it does not establish that it will take place afterwards. Let us look at other passages of the Bible where these words are used. In 2 Samuel 6:23, it says: "Michal, that daughter of Saul, had no child *until* the day of death." Does this establish, therefore, that Michal had a child *after* the day of death? Obviously not.

Psalm 110:1 prophesies about the reign of Christ the King: "Sit then at my right hand, *until* I make thy enemies thy footstool." Does this establish that *after* the defeat of the enemies of Christ that Jesus will no longer sit at the right hand of the Father? This obviously could not be the case.

Even in terms of present usage, if one were to say, "the thief refused to give back the stolen goods *before* he died," does this mean that he gave back the stolen goods *after* he died?

Therefore, the scriptural passages that state that Mary and Joseph did not come together *before* Mary was with child, in no sense establishes the fact that they did so after the birth of Christ, but simply that their coming together had not taken place before Christ's birth.

d) The term "first-born Son" neither infers nor establishes that other children were born later. In the Mosaic law the term "first-born" was applied to the child whose birth had not been *preceded* by another, regardless of whether other children followed or not. According to the Law, every mother was required to go through certain rituals after the birth of her first child (whether followed by other children or not).

Moreover, Jesus is rightly called "first-born of the Father" and "first-born of Mary." Does this infer that the Father, too, had other divine sons? Certainly not.

According to accurate scriptural exegesis and Church teaching, the perpetual virginity of Mary remains a firmly grounded doctrine.

OBJECTION 6: Objection to the Assumption of Mary

Objection: Mary had to remain in the grave after her death since death is a result of the sin that all humanity experiences (cf. Rom 3:23, 5-8; Heb 2:14-15). Therefore, Mary's bodily assumption is a human impossibility, due to her human and therefore sinful condition.

Response: As Pope Pius XII explained in the infallible definition of the Assumption in 1950, Genesis 3:15 reveals Mary, the woman and mother of the seed of victory (Jesus Christ) over Satan, as sharing in the same absolute victory in her complete opposition or "enmity" to sin. As St. Paul states, the effects of the seed of Satan (evil) are twofold: sin and death. Mary, sharing in the same enmity as her Son towards Satan's seed of evil, triumphs over sin in her Immaculate Conception and over the corruption of death in her glorious Assumption of body and soul into Heaven at the end of her earthly life.

A further distinction needs to be made regarding an accurate understanding of "death" as it results from sin. The death that takes place as a result of sin is associated with the *corruption of the body.* Jesus Christ, for example, also experienced death, but not as a result of the corruption of the body due to sin. Rather the death of Jesus consisted of a separation of soul from body on the Cross.

In regards to Mary, the Church has never officially defined the fact of her earthly death, but it remains a strong secondary tradition in the Church. What we do know is that if Mary died, it was not as a result of the corruption of the body due to sin (in light of her Immaculate Conception and sinless earthly life), but rather, as a willed acceptance of a temporary separation of soul and body in imitation of her Son as Jesus' perfect disciple.

In short, the bodily Assumption of Mary is the effect of her Immaculate Conception and a fitting close of that earthly life that ended in the same sinless state that it began, by God's unique gift and privilege.

Moreover, there is nothing in Sacred Scripture that would forbid a bodily assumption by God's power before His second coming. In fact the Gospel reference in Matthew 27:52-53 affirms its possibility: "...and the graves were opened, and many bodies arose out of them, bodies of holy men gone to their rest" (Mt 27:52).

Mary's bodily Assumption is, therefore, the appropriate conclusion of her Immaculate Conception, her sinlessness, her participation in man's redemption, and her share in Christ's glorious triumph over sin and death. It is the fitting tribute of Christ to Mary in the fulfillment of the Fourth Commandment to "honor your mother."

OBJECTION 7: Objection to Mary as Mediatrix of All Graces

Objection: How can it be said that all graces of Christ come to humanity through Mary, if we consider a) the saving graces of Christ applied to humanity before the time of the Redemption; and b) the sanctifying grace which, according to the infallible teaching of the Church, is produced automatically in the souls of those who properly receive the sacraments?

Response: a) As discussed in Chapter 3, after the Redemption of Christ, Mary distributes the graces of her Son at least as a "secondary moral cause," by her willed acts which are always subordinate and in conformity with Jesus the Redeemer and Mediator of grace.

As for those people living before the Redemption of Christ, they received graces through Mary's mediation with Mary as a "final cause." In other words, in view of the *future* merits and intercession of Mary by virtue of her participation with her Son in the world's Redemption, Mary also mediated graces to those living before the Redemption. Because Mary had an exalted participation in the Incarnation and Redemption of Jesus, which merited the graces of Redemption, she can be seen as having a secondary mediating effect in all those who receive the saving graces of Jesus, which necessarily include the saved of the Old Testament.

b) As for the sanctifying grace which the sacraments automatically confer, Mary nonetheless mediates it in several ways. First, Mary mediates the grace of the sacraments by being Mother of Jesus, the Author of Grace and the First Sacrament to the world. Secondly, Mary mediates the grace of the sacraments by her role as Co-redemptrix. By Mary's direct and meritorious participation in the Redemption of the world by Jesus Christ, she shares in the acquisition of the graces of Calvary which are distributed through the sacraments of the Church. So in this foundational and pivotal manner, Mary mediates the grace of the sacraments through her association with Christ.

Thirdly, it is through Mary's direct mediation that we receive the actual graces to desire the reception of the sacraments and to prepare us for worthy reception of the sacraments. Through Mary's direct distribution of actual graces, we receive a temporary enlightening of the mind and strengthening of the will to perform the meritorious acts of receiving the sacraments, which constitute the spiritual backbone of the Christian life. Mary's mediating presence is at every baptismal font, leading people by actual graces into the sacramental life of Jesus Christ and the Church.

Moreover, Mary's profound union with the Holy Spirit, the Sanctifier, leads to her role as Mediatrix of every grace bestowed to the human family. As St. Maximilian Kolbe taught, the Holy Spirit is so deeply united to Mary in the work of sanctification, that their inexpressible spousal union resembles (without fully reaching it) the union of the divine nature and human nature in the one person of Christ. And since the Holy Spirit always acts through the Virgin Mary in His sanctifying action, then all graces must come through Mary as Mediatrix of all graces. As St. Maximilian Kolbe describes:

The union between the Immaculata and the Holy Spirit is so inexpressible, yet so perfect, that the Holy Spirit acts only by the Most Blessed Virgin, His spouse. This is why she is the Mediatrix of all grace given by the Holy Spirit.[2]

Again, many prominent mariologists of this century (Garrigou-LaGrange, O.P., Roschini, O.S.M., Cardinal Lépicier, O.S.M., Hugan, O.P., etc.) propose Mary's physical instrumentality in the distribution of graces. One author explains Mary's mediation of the grace of the sacraments in this more proximate and direct way: "Grace begins in the Divine Nature [of Jesus], passes through the Sacred Humanity of Christ (a physical instrument), passes through Mary (also a physical instrument), and finally passes through the sacrament (also a physical instrument)."[3]

Through her foundational role as Mother of the Redeemer and Co-redemptrix, Mary's role as Mediatrix of all graces inclusively extends to the precious graces of the sacraments of the Church.

Objections to Marian Devotion

OBJECTION 8: Objection to the Rosary

Objection: The repetitious nature of the Rosary is condemned by Jesus in the Gospel where He said, "And in praying do not heap up empty phrases as the Gentiles do; for they think they will be heard for their many words" (Mt 6:7).

Response: The false type of prayer that Jesus condemns in the gospels is the heaping of "*empty phrases*." Surely, no Christian would consider the Our Father or the scriptural salutation of the Hail Mary (Lk 1:28, 42) as "empty phrases," without meaning or content.

And the legitimacy of repetitious prayer is obvious by its

unquestionable presence in Sacred Scripture. For example, Psalm 117 is completely structured upon the frequently repeated phrase: "His mercy endures for ever." So, too, is repetitious prayer an integral part of the canticle of Daniel 3:52-88, which is built upon the constantly repeated phrase, "praise and exalt him above all forever." Also, the angels give unceasing praise in the account of Heaven in the book of Revelation (cf. Rev 4:8).

The repetitious nature of the Rosary prayer (as discussed in Chapter 4) is a means of entering more deeply into the revealed Gospel mysteries of Jesus Christ thereby promoting Christian meditation. Far from being an empty repetitional structure, the peaceful repetition of the Hail Marys is an incarnational way of keeping the body focused on the disposition of the soul in order to penetrate the mysteries of Christian salvation.

What Our Lord condemns in the Gospel passage is the "empty" repetition and quantity of words that are bereft of the attention of the mind and devotion of the heart. The Rosary is vocal and mental prayer form that utilizes a *prayerful* repetition of the Gospel-based Our Father and Hail Mary and has no intrinsic connection with the "heaping of empty phrases" condemned by Christ.

But it is important to remember that every prayer form can be abused by a type of formalism that practices the external act without the proper internal intention of the heart to "communicate with the One whom you know loves you," in the words of St. Teresa.

When the Rosary is used as an authentic form of Christian vocal prayer and meditation and is prayer with the proper internal disposition of love of God, necessary for any true Christian prayer form, it is then a litany-like succession of Hail Marys that, in the words of Pope Paul VI, "becomes in itself an unceasing praise of Christ."

OBJECTION 9: Objection Against Consecration to Jesus Through Mary

Objection: The act of Marian consecration involves a) giving oneself entirely to Mary, and this constitutes an act of adoration; now a Christian is only permitted to give himself entirely to God and never to a creature; and b) giving all our merits and good works to Jesus through Mary will make us spiritually incapable of helping the souls of our parents, relatives and friends.

Response: a) Here again a distinction must be made between acts of "latria" and "dulia" (see Chapter 1). Consecration to God, for example, to the Sacred Heart of Jesus, is an act in the order of latria, which is the worship paid exclusively to God, and in which a person is given directly and completely to God.

Consecration to Mary (for example, to her Immaculate Heart) is an analogous act in the order of hyperdulia, that exalted devotion which the Mother of God properly deserves. Here a person gives himself entirely to Mary *as a means* of union with Jesus Christ. Giving oneself entirely to Mary does not mean that Mary is the goal or final recipient of the self-gift; but rather, that it is a Christ-designated means of consecrating oneself to Jesus and renewing one's baptismal vows. One's gift of self to Mary in the order of hyperdulia, or exalted veneration, is the best means to a complete and total gift of self to Christ in the order of adoration, which is proper only for Our Lord.

b) To the objection that through Marian consecration we lose our spiritual ability to aid the souls of our parents, relatives, and friends, St. Louis Marie de Montfort offers the following clear and succinct answer:

> It is not credible that our parents, friends and benefactors should suffer from the fact of our being devoted and

consecrated without exception to the service of Our Lord and His Holy Mother. To think this would be to think unworthily of the goodness and power of Jesus and Mary, who know well how to assist our parents, friends and benefactors, out of our own little spiritual revenue or by others.[4]

De Montfort's response reflects the spiritual humility all Christians should have in regards to their limited ability to dispense properly their own spiritual benefits, in contrast to the best and perfect distribution of graces made by Jesus and Mary. Further, we must remain assured that total consecration to Jesus through Mary will result only in a greater obedience to the commandments of God, including the Fourth Commandment to "honor your father and mother" and the Gospel command to "love your neighbor."

OBJECTION 10: Objection Against Marian Private Revelation

Objection: How can any human being, including Mary, appear after death in a way only possible by God Himself?

Response: Again, we return to the distinction between "being God" and "participating in the power of God." Mary, especially since she is not bound by the limits of time and space in Heaven, can participate in God's power to become visible to a person on earth, to communicate, and even to be present in her assumed body in a type of three dimensional apparition. Scripture attests to a vision or apparition by persons who have died and have risen in Christ; this is recorded in Matthew 27:52-53: "...and the graves were opened and many bodies arose out of them, bodies of holy men gone to their rest; who, after his rising again, left their graves and went into the holy city, where they *were seen by many.*" If the dead who rise in Christ can appear in bodily form to others, certainly the Mother of Jesus, whose body is gloriously assumed into Heaven, can appear to her earthly children with Gospel messages encouraging greater faith, prayer, penance, conversion and peace (See Chapter 6 for full treatment on Marian private revelation).

Conclusion

It is our hope that the explanations provided in this chapter, as well as the contents of the book in general, have provided some theological and reasonable grounds for a full acceptance and appreciation of Mary's role in God's drama of human salvation, a maternal role that hopefully will evoke a sincere filial Christian love on the part of her earthly children.

We end this work with the words that ended the Second Vatican Council's profound treatment on Mary. It is a prayer of petition that beseeches the most powerful intercession of the Mother of God for the unity of all her earthly children into the one Church of Christ:

The entire body of the faithful pours forth urgent supplications to the Mother of God and of men that she, who aided the beginnings of the Church by her prayers, may now, exalted as she is above all the angels and saints, intercede before her Son in the fellowship of all the saints, until all families of people, whether they are honored with the title of Christian or whether they still do not know the Saviour, may be happily gathered together in peace and harmony into one People of God, for the glory of the Most Holy and Undivided Trinity (*Lumen Gentium*, No. 69).

Notes

1. Henry Cardinal Newman, *Inspiration in its Relation to Revelation*, 1884; cf. Karl Keating, *Catholicism and Fundamentalism*, (San Francisco: Ignatius Press) Ch. 10.
2. Fr. H. M. Manteau-Bonamy, O.P., *Immaculate Conception and the Holy Spirit: The Marian Teachings of Fr. Kolbe*, (Kenosha, WI: Franciscan Marytown Press, 1977). Letter to Father Milolajczyk, July 28, 1935, p.99.
3. William Most, *Mary in Our Life*, (New York: Kenedy and Sons, 1954) p.38.
4. De Montfort, *True Devotion*, I. art. 2, No. 132.

Appendix

How to Pray the Rosary

The Rosary is a form of vocal and mental prayer on the mysteries of our Redemption, divided into fifteen decades. The recitation of each decade is accompanied by meditation on one of the fifteen events or "mysteries."

1. "The Sign of the Cross" and "Apostles' Creed"

2. "Our Father"

3. Three "Hail Marys"

4. "Glory Be"; announce first mystery.

5. "Our Father"

6. Ten "Hail Marys"; meditate on the mystery announced.

7. "Glory Be" and optional "Fatima Prayer"

8. Announce second mystery and repeat as in 5, 6, 7. Continue in like manner until the five mysteries are prayed.

9. "Hail, Holy Queen," "Rosary Prayer"; end with "The Sign of the Cross"

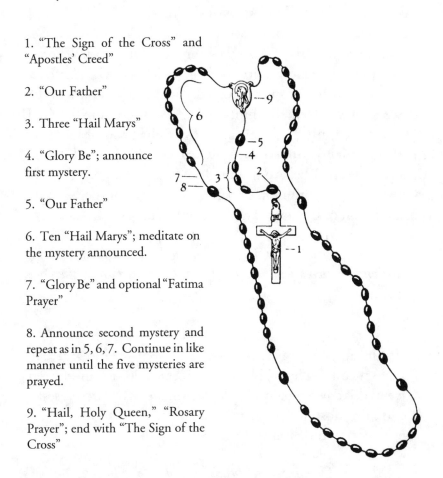

(Rosary diagram used with permission of The Riehle Foundation.)

We begin the Rosary by holding the Cross, the sign of our Faith, and making the Sign of the Cross as we pray:

The Sign of the Cross

In the name of the Father, and of the Son, and of the Holy Spirit. Amen.

While still holding the Cross we profess our beliefs as we pray:

The Apostles' Creed

I believe in God, the Father Almighty, Creator of Heaven and earth; and in Jesus Christ, His only Son, Our Lord; Who was conceived by the Holy Spirit, born of the Virgin Mary, suffered under Pontius Pilate, was crucified, died, and was buried. He descended into Hell; the third day He rose again from the dead; He ascended into Heaven, sits at the right hand of God, the Father Almighty; from thence He shall come to judge the living and the dead. I believe in the Holy Spirit, the holy Catholic Church, the communion of Saints, the forgiveness of sins, the resurrection of the body, and life everlasting. Amen.

On the first bead we pray the prayer Jesus taught us. This is traditionally offered for the intention of the Holy Father, the Pope. We pray:

Our Father

Our Father, Who art in Heaven, hallowed be Thy name; Thy kingdom come; Thy will be done on earth, as it is in Heaven. Give us this day our daily bread; and forgive us our trespasses, as we forgive those who trespass against us; and lead us not into temptation, but deliver us from evil. Amen.

On each of the next three beads we invoke our Blessed Mother's intercession for an increase in the virtues of faith, hope and love as we pray:

Hail Mary

Hail, Mary, full of grace; the Lord is with thee; blessed art thou among women, and blessed is the fruit of thy womb, Jesus. Holy Mary, Mother of God, pray for us sinners, now and at the hour of our death. Amen.

We follow the three Hail Marys with a prayer of praise of the Most Holy Trinity as we pray (no bead):

Glory Be

Glory be to the Father, and to the Son, and to the Holy Spirit. As it was in the beginning, is now, and ever shall be, world without end. Amen.

On the fifth bead we *announce the first mystery (see list of mysteries below) and while meditating on the mystery say one Our Father and ten Hail Marys (one on each of the next ten beads) and a Glory Be (no bead). Then, as requested by Our Lady of the Rosary at Fatima, we may pray:

Fatima Prayer

O my Jesus, forgive us our sins, save us from the fires of Hell, lead all souls to Heaven, especially those who are most in need of Thy mercy.

(Repeat from * above for each mystery.)

We may close our Rosary with:

Hail, Holy Queen

Hail, Holy Queen, Mother of Mercy, our life, our sweetness and our hope. To thee do we cry, poor banished children of Eve;

to thee do we send up our sighs, mourning and weeping in this valley of tears. Turn then, most gracious Advocate, thine eyes of mercy toward us; and after this our exile show unto us the blessed fruit of thy womb, Jesus. O clement, O loving, O sweet Virgin Mary:

V. Pray for us, O holy Mother of God.

R. That we may be made worthy of the promises of Christ.

Rosary Prayer (optional)

O God, whose only-begotten Son, by His life, death and resurrection has purchased for us the rewards of eternal life; grant, we beseech you, that meditating on these mysteries of the most holy Rosary of the Blessed Virgin Mary, we may imitate what they contain, and obtain what they promise. Through the same Christ our Lord. Amen. (From the Roman Ritual)

End with The Sign of the Cross.

The Fifteen Mysteries of the Most Holy Rosary

Joyful

1. The Annunciation — "Hail, full of grace, the Lord is with thee. Blessed art thou among women" (Lk 1:28).

2. The Visitation — "When Elizabeth heard the greeting of Mary the babe in her womb leapt, and she was filled with the Holy Spirit" (Lk 1:41).

3. The Birth of Jesus — "And she brought forth her first-born Son and wrapped him in swaddling clothes" (Lk 2:7).

4. The Presentation — "According to the law of Moses, they took Jesus up to Jerusalem to present him to the Lord" (Lk 2:22).

5. The Finding of the Child Jesus in the Temple — "After three days they found him in the temple. He was sitting in the midst of the teachers" (Lk 2:46).

Sorrowful

6. The Agony in the Garden — "Jesus came with them to Gethsemane and he began to be saddened and exceedingly troubled" (Mt 26:36).

7. The Scourging at the Pillar — "Pilate then took Jesus and had him scourged" (Jn 19:1).

8. The Crowning of Thorns — "And plaiting a crown of thorns they put it upon his head and a reed into his right hand" (Mt 27:29).

9. Jesus Carries the Cross — "And bearing the Cross for himself, he went forth to the place called The Skull" (Jn 19:17).

10. The Crucifixion — "And when they came to the place called The Skull they crucified him" (Lk 23:33).

Glorious

11. The Resurrection — "He is not here, but has risen. Behold the place where they laid him" (Lk 24:6; Mk 16:6).

12. The Ascension — "And he was taken up into Heaven and sits at the right hand of God" (Mk 16:19).

13. The Descent of the Holy Spirit — "And suddenly there came a sound from Heaven...and there appeared to them parted tongues...and they were filled with the Holy Spirit" (Acts 2:2, 3,4).

14. The Assumption of Mary, Body and Soul into Heaven — "Hear, O daughter, and see; turn your ear, for the King shall desire your beauty. All glorious is the king's daughter as she enters: her raiment is threaded with spun gold" (Ps 45:11,12,14).

15. The Coronation of Mary, Queen of Heaven and Earth — "And a great sign appeared in Heaven: a woman clothed with the sun, and the moon under her feet, and upon her head a crown of twelve stars" (Rev 12:1).

If five decades a day are said, the general rule is that the Joyful Mysteries are said on Monday and Thursday, the Sorrowful Mysteries on Tuesday and Friday, and the Glorious Mysteries on Wednesday and Saturday. On Sundays during Advent the Joyful Mysteries are said, on Sundays during Lent the Sorrowful, and the Glorious Mysteries are said on all other Sundays.

Marian Prayers

Sub Tuum Praesidium

We fly to your patronage,
O Holy Mother of God,
despise not our petitions
in our necessities,
but deliver us from all danger,
O ever glorious and blessed Virgin.

Alma Redemptoris

Loving mother of the Redeemer,
gate of heaven, star of the sea,
assist your people who have fallen yet strive to rise again.
To the wonderment of nature you bore your Creator,
yet remained a virgin after as before.
You who received Gabriel's joyful greeting,
have pity on us poor sinners.

(or in Latin)

Alma Redemptoris Mater, quae pervia caeli
porta manes, et stella maris, succurre cadenti,
surgere qui curat, populo: tu quae genuisti,
natura mirante, tuum sanctum Genitorem,
Virgo prius ac posterius, Gabrielis ab ore
sumens illud Ave, peccatorum miserere.

Memorare

Remember, O most gracious Virgin Mary,
that never was it known
that anyone who fled to your protection,
implored your help or sought your intercession,
was left unaided.

Inspired with this confidence,
I fly to you, O Virgin of virgins, my Mother;
to you do I come,
before you I stand, sinful and sorrowful.
O Mother of the Word Incarnate,
despise not my petitions,
but in your mercy hear and answer me.

Angelus

V. The Angel of the Lord declared unto Mary.
R. And she conceived of the Holy Spirit.
Hail Mary...

V. Behold the handmaid of the Lord.
R. Be it done unto me according to Thy word.
Hail Mary...

V. And the Word was made flesh.
R. And dwelt among us.
Hail Mary...

Let us pray:
Pour forth we beseech Thee, O Lord, Thy grace into our hearts,
that we to whom the Incarnation of Christ, Thy Son, was made

known by the message of an angel, may by His passion and cross be brought to the glory of His resurrection, through the same Christ Our Lord. Amen.

Queen of Heaven
(replaces the Angelus during the Easter Season)

Queen of Heaven, rejoice, alleluia:
For He whom you merited to bear, alleluia,
Has risen, as He said, alleluia.
Pray for us to God, alleluia.

V. Rejoice and be glad, O Virgin Mary, alleluia.
R. Because the Lord is truly risen, alleluia.

Let us pray.

O God,
who by the resurrection of Your Son,
Our Lord Jesus Christ,
granted joy to the whole world:
grant, we beg You,
that through the intercession of the Virgin Mary, His Mother,
we may lay hold of the joys of eternal life.
Through the same Christ our Lord. Amen.

Ave Regina Caelorum

Ave, Regina Caelorum,
ave, Domina angelorum,
salve, radix, salve, porta,
ex qua mundo lux est orta.

Gaude, Virgo gloriosa,
super omnes speciosa;
vale, o valde decora,
et pro nobis Christum exora.

The Litany of Loreto

Lord, have mercy.
Christ, have mercy.
Lord, have mercy.

Christ, hear us.
Christ, graciously hear us.
God, the Father of Heaven,
have mercy on us.
God the Son, Redeemer of the world,
have mercy on us.
God the Holy Spirit,
have mercy on us.
Holy Trinity, one God.
have mercy on us.

Holy Mary,
pray for us. (repeat after each invocation)
Mother of Christ,
Mother of the Church,
Mother of divine grace,
Mother most pure,
Mother most chaste,
Mother inviolate,
Mother undefiled,
Mother most amiable,
Mother most admirable,

Mother of good counsel,
Mother of our Creator,
Mother of our Savior,
Virgin most prudent,
Virgin most venerable,
Virgin most renowned,
Virgin most powerful,
Virgin most merciful,
Virgin most faithful,
Mirror of justice,
Seat of wisdom,
Cause of our joy,
Spiritual vessel,
Vessel of honor,
Singular vessel of devotion,
Mystical rose,
Tower of David,
Tower of ivory,
House of gold,
Ark of the covenant,
Gate of Heaven,
Morning star,
Health of the sick,
Refuge of sinners,
Comforter of the afflicted,
Help of Christians,
Queen of angels,
Queen of patriarchs,
Queen of prophets,
Queen of apostles,
Queen of martyrs,
Queen of confessors,
Queen of virgins,
Queen of all saints,

Queen conceived without Original Sin,
Queen assumed into Heaven,
Queen of the most holy Rosary,
Queen of peace,

Lamb of God, You take away the sins of the world;
spare us, O Lord.
Lamb of God, You take away the sins of the world;
graciously hear us, O Lord.
Lamb of God, You take away the sins of the world;
have mercy on us.

V. Pray for us, O Holy Mother of God.
R. *That we may be made worthy of the promises of Christ.*

Let us pray.

Grant, we beg you, O Lord God,
that we your servants
may enjoy lasting health of mind and body,
and by the glorious intercession
of the Blessed Mary, ever Virgin,
be delivered from present sorrow
and enter into the joy of eternal happiness.
Through Christ our Lord.
R. *Amen*

Index

Thérèse of Lisieux, St., 16
Tradition, Sacred (nature and role
     of), *2-5*, 132
True Devotion to Mary, 16, 110,
     118, 120

U

Uncreated Immaculate Concep-
     tion, 81, 116

V

Vatican Council II:
     teachings on Mary (see *Lumen
          Gentium*)
veneration:
     of Mary, 2, 11, 12, 14, 159;
     of Saints, 10, 11, 14, 16, 159
visionary (defined), 136
Visitation, The, 67, 82

W

Ward, J. Neville, 105
World War I, 103, 43, 146
World War II, 146